MANAGING WORK AND
RELATIONSHIPS AT 35,000 FEET

MANAGING WORK AND RELATIONSHIPS AT 35,000 FEET

A Practical Guide For Making Personal Life Fit Aircrew Shift Work, Jetlag, And Absences From Home

Dr. Carina Eriksen

Chartered Counselling Psychologist

KARNAC

First published in 2009 by
Karnac Books Ltd
118 Finchley Road
London NW3 5HT

British Library Cataloguing in Publication Data

A C.I.P. for this book is available from the British Library

ISBN-13: 978-1-85575-578-9

Typeset by Vikatan Publishing Solutions (p) Ltd., Chennai, India

Printed in Great Britain

www.karnacbooks.com

CONTENTS

ACKNOWLEDGEMENT

I am enormously grateful to the following people who have helped at the various stages of this project and in the production of the book: Professor Robert Bor of the Royal Free Hospital, my clinical and research 'mentor' for the past four years, helped to develop the original ideas and has provided extensive support throughout; Martin Casey provided additional contributions and ideas; Ceilidh offered extensive editorial assistance. Lastly, this book would not have come about without the many conversations I have had with cabin crew and pilots from various airlines across the world. I would like to thank the many crew whose willingness to share their experience of work and personal living inspired me to write this book.

ABOUT THE AUTHOR

Dr Carina Eriksen is a Chartered Counselling Psychologist with many years experience of the Cabin Crew profession. She holds a BSc Honours in Psychology, a Master's degree in Psychology from London Metropolitan University and a Doctorate in Counselling Psychology. Carina works in the NHS as well as in private practice. She provides therapy to adults, adolescents, children, and families drawing on her speciality within Cognitive Behavioural Therapy and Systemic orientations. She also offers psychological support within organisational settings, including stress management and work-life conflict. She is a visiting lecturer on the MSc in Air Transport Management at City University. Carina has carried out research on sleep deprivation and aircrew relationships. She has worked as a long-haul cabin crew member for a major UK airline for nearly 11 years. Carina started flying shortly after completing her A Levels in the North of Norway. Her work has been published in books and scientific journals. She is a Chartered member of the British Psychological Society.

Managing work and relationships at 35,000 feet

The popular image and perceived lifestyle of an airline pilot or flight attendant is such that makes it hard for some people to understand the nature and extent of stress and disruption to the lives of air crew. Every day, millions of passengers worldwide place their lives in the capable hands of air crew. They rightly expect air crew to be highly professional and experienced in their respective roles and proficient in their unique tasks. They take it for granted that pilots and flight attendants manage the challenges of the job, such as jet lag, fatigue, disrupted personal relationships, stressed, fearful and demanding passengers, and do not let any of these challenges affect their safety.

Dr. Carina Eriksen—herself a senior flight attendant as well as a highly experienced counselling psychologist—has studied the work patterns and lifestyle challenges to air crew and delved deeply into the emotional, cognitive and behavioural aspects of surviving and thriving psychologically as a pilot or flight attendant. This book, the first of its kind to address these sensitive topics, presents a fascinating insight into how air crew can best cope with their unique lifestyles. Based on real life situations and examples of problems discussed by air crew, she has set out to identify what problems they face and how best to cope with or overcome them.

The book is thoroughly practical, free from abstract and difficult to understand psychological terms or 'psychobabble'. It conveys a positive message that informed crew can enjoy better physical and mental health, can cope better with the job and improve their personal lives. Martin Casey, himself an experienced airline pilot, contributes a section on improving physical health and the role of exercise. Dr. Eriksen also describes how and where crew members can find specialist medical and psychological support and help if they need it.

As the editor for this series of Karnac self help books, it gives me great pleasure to introduce this highly practical and insightful new title. 'Managing Work and Relationships at 35,000 feet' is essential reading for pilots and flight attendants around the world, whether they fly short- or long-haul. This book will prove to be a valuable tool for those who work in the airline and travel industry, as well as their families, friends and loved ones who often bear the greatest burden in terms of disruption to their lives. It will also appeal to those who train flight and cabin crew, aviation human resources specialists, therapists and psychologists, as well as doctors and nurses who work in the airline industry.

Professor Robert Bor DPhil CPsychol CSci
FBPsS UKCP Reg FRAeS
Consultant Clinical Psychologist and
Specialist in Aviation Psychology
Royal Free Hospital, London

INTRODUCTION

The aviation industry is one of the world largest employers; there are millions of people who work for various airlines across the world. Cabin crew and pilots constitute a vital part of the airline workforce, especially in terms of ensuring airline safety and providing customer service. As frontline personnel they are often thought of as 'the face' of the airline industry. This has become especially the case when considering how recent technological developments have allowed the consumer market to enjoy wholly computerised ticketing and check-in facilities. As such, the aircrew community has for many passengers become the first, and perhaps the only, point of 'real' physical contact with an airline representative. Surprisingly little has been published on the work roles and lifestyle of this group of workers, although, where available, literature appears across a diversity of dramatised sitcoms (e.g. Mile High, 2003) and Media articles. This book provides a realistic, informed and modern version of the aircrew profession and provides suggestions, based on research and experience, on how to cope with disruption to one's personal life.

The main focus of recent literature in the field of aviation psychology has been on safety and the medical implications of air travel. Emerging issues such as terrorism, airline accidents and unruly passenger behaviour have broadened the agenda for aviation psychologist. At the same time, the possibility of longer non-stop travel and the introduction of the new Airbus 380 with a licence to carry up to 800 passengers calls for a shift in the working environment with increased pressure on aircrew workers. This book seeks to contribute to a psychological perspective to aircrew wellbeing and help aircrew to acquire an understanding of how to better manage the many challenges arising from sleep deprivation and frequent absence from friends and loved others at home.

This book is written mainly for cabin crew and pilots, others who work professionally with the aircrew community, as well as those who have a personal interest in aircrew wellbeing. This includes airline managers, aviation psychologists, aircrew partners, family, and their friends. A further audience includes researchers, medical professionals, and clinical and occupational psychologists.

The inspiration to write this book arose from a combination of personal interest in the crew lifestyle and extensive research in the field. I have worked as long haul crew for a major UK airline for many years. I know what it feels like to constantly miss out on important events with significant others, to have limited control over my work schedule, and to sacrifice sleep in order to try and maintain 'a social life' at home. At times I have felt guilty and homesick when being absent from birthday parties, school reunions and christenings. I have also experienced frustration and exhaustion following the countless episodes of jetlag and fatigue. These are only some of the many challenges that constitute the reality of the aircrew lifestyle. Sadly, these aspects of the job are often those that are overlooked by the media who sometimes seek to glamorise the work. Consequently, there is little serious insight is known into the everyday lives of aircrew except for those who have direct experience of the job itself. This means that crew are often deprived of the wider recognition, support, and understanding they perhaps deserve. This book seeks to rectify this on two accounts. Firstly, it seeks to identify the psychological adversity faced by crew who are often away from home for long periods of time. Secondly, the book draws on extensive psychological research about how crew cope with sleep deprivation, low work control, as well as professional, social, and intimate relationships. This knowledge has been translated into useful and 'easy to follow' techniques for coping with the influence of work demands on personal living. It is hoped that readers can assimilate such learning into their already extensive repertoire of combating work-life inferences.

Psychology is not a precise science, however, and it is not possible to predict how crew may cope with the various challenges presented by their somewhat unique lifestyle. There are too many factors and variables that elude such precision, in particular individual differences in coping styles, mental health, culture, age, historical background, personal characteristics, social network and biological pre-dispositions amongst the many thousands of crew across the world. This is reflected in the structure of the book as the guidelines in each chapter are intended to provide useful hints that represent the wide diversity of people currently working as professional aircrew.

The book does not offer an exhaustive list of topics on aircrew requirements nor do the contents prescribe how to best overcome the various psychological challenges faced by crew. Instead, through the unique combination of insight and experience of the crew lifestyle and as a practising psychologist, I seek to raise awareness and establish the important benefits of learning how psychology and 'common sense' can help crew themselves to deal with work stress, relationship difficulties, and sleep deprivation. I am aware that there are gaps in this text and that many other topics could have been included. I hope that readers of the book will provide feedback and that future editions will incorporate and reflect their ideas and suggestions.

The chapters that follow address a range of topics concerning aircrew psychological wellbeing and coping and have been arranged around certain themes. In Chapter 1, the scene is set by highlighting the unique aspects of aircrew roles and responsibilities. Although it is thought that the work requirements of the flight crew community may differ from that of the cabin crew workforce, especially with regard to technical and operational knowledge, it is important to emphasise that both groups share an equally demanding lifestyle. A distinction is also made between short-haul and long-haul operations as each group of workers is thought to experience different kinds of work requirements with the former being more prone to 'early morning starts and late night finishes', jetlag, long duty hours, and night flights.

Chapter 2 aims to identify the emotional, cognitive and, to a lesser degree, physical symptoms of jetlag and fatigue. I discuss how sleep deprivation can disrupt aircrews' 'natural' ability to think, perceive, concentrate, perform, make decisions, as well as to process their emotions. The chapter does not attempt to prescribe set ways of dealing with sleep difficulties. Instead, it recognises that home demands, whether seeing friends, family, or a partner can often interfere with crews' capacity to gain adequate sleep prior to and in-between long duty hours at work.

In the next three chapters we will look at aircrew relationships, both at work and home. Relationships are central to most people's lives and are time-consuming. We engage with people at different levels on a daily basis. At the simplest level we interact with other people when we visit the bank, go shopping, or join a fitness class and even during such basic activities form some level of relationships with them. Most people are also engaged in more important relationships; with colleagues at work, family members, friends and partners. Such interactions and relationships are important for both physical and emotional wellbeing. People who are excessively isolated and lonely are prone to negative feelings, such as sadness and depression, and may also suffer negative effects on their physical health. The next three chapters will examine home and work relationships for aircrew. Crew face unique challenges with relationships, repeatedly making and breaking them while travelling. Feelings of instability can result. When these are compounded by an exhausting lifestyle and the pressures of managing social and family commitments, the entire social system of the aircrew population may suffer. For more vulnerable and less experienced crew members, these pressures can be particularly challenging. Even for more experienced crew, frequent absences from family and friends can disrupt intimate relationships. A commitment to the kind of lifestyle required to be an aircrew member means juggling priorities and making sacrifices that can affect formation and maintenance of personal relationships.

In chapter 3, aircrew group dynamics both onboard and off the aircraft are outlined. The act of travelling with a new set of colleagues every time one reports for work often leads to brief and/or short-lasting relations at work. Crew are constantly engaged in a process of forming and breaking professional relationships and this can lead to a sense of loneliness even for the more resilient type of crew member. The topic of relationships is also the central focus of Chapter 4. The frequent absences from home can further complicate crews' ability to form and maintain social relationships. Whilst it is recognised that the size of one's social network and desire for social interactions at home may differ from one crew member to another, the importance of time management, prioritisation, and decision making when attempting to 'juggle' work requirements with social living is emphasised. In Chapter 5, a different kind of relationship is presented to the reader, namely that of marriage or a partnership. For many people, personal relationships may be regarded as the most important ones. This is also reflected in the psychological literature as close and supportive relationships can often act as a buffer against psychological illness. On the other hand, relationship difficulties such as conflict or a separation can generate emotional disruptions for each partner involved. When this is compounded by broken relationships at work, there may be limited support for aircrew across both the home and the work domain.

In chapter 6, the emphasis is on the overall task of dealing with the simultaneous pressure of sleep deprivation, daily chores, and social/personal relationships. Although each of these single factors may generate stress for the individual crew member, their combined effect is thought to present the strongest challenge to aircrew psychological wellbeing. This chapter provides a range of preventative techniques that seeks, one hopes, to help crew improve their work-life balance.

Without reference to the health challenges faced by aircrew, this book would not have been complete. In Chapter 7, Martin Casey offers an insight into crew's physical wellbeing, drawing from a combination of available literature and personal experience in the field. Who is better to write about this topic than an experienced commercial airline pilot, triathlete, and sport enthusiast with a specific interest in both the mental and physical health benefits of exercise?

Chapter 8 offers a brief historical view of the aircrew profession along with a discussion of the aircrew recruitment process. This chapter is mainly intended for those who wish to pursue a career as either cabin crew or flight crew and therefore differs from the preceding ones. Having read about how aircrew cope with the challenges of the job, prospective aircrew may either be motivated or deterred from applying to work in the airline industry. The Chapter may also be of benefit to existing flyers who are interested in recruiting for their respective employer.

CHAPTER ONE

The aircrew role

Some people have stereotypical views about the aircrew profession. This chapter addresses some of the more common misconceptions, particularly those relating to a lifestyle of permanent holidays, partying, drinking, and sunbathing. Aircrew speak about the hardship of maintaining relationships with non-flyers, who may find it hard to understand the reality of the crew lifestyle.

Problems associated with the job include:

- Irregular work patterns beyond the control of the individual which mean unavoidable difficulties with forward planning and commitments;
- Jetlag, cumulative sleep deprivation and fatigue from frequently crossing time zones;
- Limited time to spend at home means difficulties with developing and maintaining social/family relations, partnerships, and keeping on top of everyday tasks;
- Restricted opportunities to form long and lasting relationships with colleagues because of frequently changing work teams.

Stereotypes and the media

The respectability of the airline profession has been challenged recently by media reports of irresponsible behaviour by pilots. On the 4th of July 2002, BBC News reported on two US commercial pilots who faced charges of flying under the influence of alcohol. On June 24th 2005, a Norwegian court sentenced a British Airway's pilot for preparing to fly even though members of his crew were drunk. The hype surrounding these stories may have damaged the reputation of the aircrew community at large, fuelling stereotypical views of party driven lifestyle filled with constant shopping, drinking, and sunbathing. Aircrew are often portrayed in this way through TV sitcoms such as in a recent series on Sky, Mile High (2003–2005). The series focuses on the tales of an irresponsible crew from a fictitious airline 'Fresh', based at Stanstead airport. The lack of professionalism they show both onboard the aircraft and in their social lives could be mistaken for troubled teenage high school living. Though the majority of crew are professional, earnest individuals, they must often defend their reputation or educate people about the realities of their lives as these stereotypes may be all that non-flyers know about them.

The realities of the profession

Being an aircrew member offers an opportunity to travel. The glamour associated with this is one of the primary attractions of the job. Every day presents new experiences, be they a new destination, irregular hours of work or the ever changing complement of people to work with. The routine procedures that crew must follow when on board does provide some secure regularity within their jobs. Typically, a duty period starts with a briefing before take off. This is often the first time crew get to meet the colleagues they will be working with on that flight. The main aim of the briefing is to ensure that everyone is aware of the safety requirements and will act competently in case of an emergency, to allocate working positions, to discuss relevant details of the destination, and to encourage team bonding. A briefing for pilots may provide additional relevant details such as weather conditions, routing, and technical instructions pertaining to the aircraft operation.

Once onboard, cabin crew and pilots immediately begin to prepare for the flight before the first passengers are allowed to board the aircraft. Pilots perform a range of safety and security checks to ensure that technical, medical, and related aircraft equipment is intact and working to the expected standard. In the mean time, cabin crew are busy checking that there is enough food to keep customers comfortable throughout the flight. On the flight deck, the pilots engage with engineers, air traffic controllers, baggage loaders and the aircraft dispatcher to negotiate departure times and to oversee aircraft operation. The captain is ultimately responsible for the safety and security of the entire flight process. During the boarding, cabin crew, apart from meeting and greeting passengers, are responsible for dealing with seat changes, drunkenness, flight delays, or any other problems that could affect safety or impact on customer experience. Depending on the size of the aircraft and length of the journey, the cabin crew usually consists of 4–10 main crew members, 2–4 'pursers' who are in charge of a delegated cabin (e.g. economy class, business class, first class), and a senior cabin crew member who directs the overall passenger service and continuously updates the captain. Uncertainty about responsibilities can compromise passenger and aircraft safety, and it is a requirement of the European Joint Aviation Authority that duties and roles are pre-specified before take off. Most airlines have a 'chain of command' that clearly puts the operating captain in charge with his or her co-pilot as the second in command. They are followed by the senior cabin crew member, then the most experienced purser and so on. On longer routes it is sometimes necessary to have an additional set of pilots on board. The 'reserve' captain, as opposed to the operating co-pilot, will then become second in command while the reserve co-pilot is fourth in the chain, ahead of the senior cabin crew member.

When the seatbelt sign is switched off after take off, the in-flight service commences, usually a drinks and meal service with light snacks on full service journeys. Crew undertake frequent security checks throughout the flight to minimise the risk to safety and to reduce fire hazards. They also observe passenger behaviour and wellbeing. The tragic events of 9/11 have changed the set up on board an aircraft. There is now restricted access to the flight deck as a precaution against terrorist attacks and hijacking. Admission to the cockpit is quite restricted. Communication with the pilots is primarily through internal telephones located throughout the plane, although crew can enter the flight deck if necessary, e.g. for refreshments, medical attention, or pressing security matters. The recent flight deck door policy improves safety for everyone onboard, but it means that pilots are confined to a small, more cramped environment, often for long periods of time.

After landing, when the passengers have disembarked, crew make their way through immigration and customs and are transported to their appointed hotel for the duration of their layover. On shorter routes, the layover is usually less than 24 hours while on longer routes it can vary between 1 and 9 days. The exact work schedules for crew depend upon commercial routing and how the particular airline allocates staff. Some employers have additional shuttles within Europe, the United States, or between Far Eastern countries, while other airlines seek to limit long haul crew to a single destination on a duty. Airlines that run additional shuttles, although requiring their staff to commit to longer periods away from home, usually reward them with longer intervals between duty periods. Quick 'turnarounds' required on short haul trips mean that crew often fly out and return in the same day and don't have to spend as much time away from home.

In their layover periods, crew are free to enjoy what their destinations have to offer. It is this perk that often attracts people to the job. There are plenty of opportunities to sight-see, shop, visit restaurants etc. in countries across the globe. Some airlines offer discounted travel for staff which they can use to explore further afield during their longer layover periods. For example, a crew member travelling to Kuala Lumpur in Malaysia may wish to escape the city, to a nearby island such as Langkawi or Pangkor. Likewise, travels to Los Angeles in California provide an ideal opportunity for crew to visit Las Vegas for a day or two, which can easily be accessed either by car, plane, or a bus journey. On shorter layovers, there are opportunities to travel to nearby desti-nations, such as a day trip to the Alps if staying in Geneva. Most hotels have a fully equipped gym open 24 hours a day. The hotel concierge, for example, can assist with details on local running routes, hiking tracks, or popular cycling paths if necessary. Other individuals prioritise sleep during their layovers, particularly if there are pressing engagements waiting at home. If you are employed in the industry, here are some tips to help you enjoy the opportunities presented by your travel:

- Engage with the local surroundings. Make an effort to see what's on offer and to experience the culture of local people at your destination.
- The Lonely Planet guides provide details of local attractions. Using this you can plan your adventures and organise your visits in advance.
- Ensure you get enough rest before flying home.
- However, don't spend too much time on your own as you may feel bored, lonely and homesick.
- Use your short layovers to improve your fitness level. Regular exercise improves physical and mental wellbeing and may help you manage fatigue.

- Consider going out with a colleague if you feel anxious about being alone in a foreign place.
- Set yourself personal goals during your layovers. These might include socialising, working through ones shopping list, visiting a museum, catching up on sleep, reading a novel, studying for an exam, or keeping fit. Achieving these will give you a focus and a sense of self accomplishment. In the long term this can enhance your motivation and job satisfaction.

It's important to consider your personal safety at all times. No cities on earth are crime free and being vigilant can help to prevent theft and other possible harmful events. Be sensible when eating and drinking in countries that run a high risk of food and water contamination, such as in parts of South America, destinations in the Far East, India, Africa, Eastern Europe and the Middle East.

Consider these tips to enhance your personal safety:

- Don't carry visible jewellery when visiting cities with high crime rates. An expensive looking ring, necklace, watch, camera, or mobile phone can attract unwanted attention.
- Leave your valuable possessions, such as identification documents, passports, computers, ipods, cash etc. in the hotel. Most hotel rooms have a safety box in the room for your use. If this is not the case, consider using your suitcase for safe keeping as most modern luggage devices offers a lockable alternative.
- Be sensible with your clothes; choose an outfit that is sensitive to the local culture.
- Never leave your drink unattended. It only takes a second for it to be spiked. Drugs that are used for this include GHB, Rohypnol and Ketamine, which you may not notice in your drink. Effects include 'blackouts', impaired judgment and functioning, blurred vision and memory

loss which may last for hours depending on the type and dose of the drug. During these periods you will be vulnerable to exploitation.
- Drink bottled water and make sure the seal is intact before you drink it.
- Avoid buying food from local street vendors in countries that are known for low hygiene standards. If you can, avoid food types such as shellfish, cold salads or undercooked meat as these carry an increased risk of food poisoning, vomiting, and/or diarrhoea.

Shift work, fatigue and absences from home

The opportunity to travel, and to meet a range of different peoples and cultures is often what attracts people to the job as pilots or crew. However, in surveys, UK based crew revealed that behind their 'plastic' smiles and groomed façade there were real conflicts in balancing home and work life, difficulties with professional and personal relationships and a demanding mix of interpersonal and intrapersonal skills required. The realities of the job, such as a lack of control over lifestyle, being away from family and friends and the difficulties with planning ahead were negative points. There are also physical challenges associated with aircraft travel, including sleep deprivation, jetlag, and dehydration.

Crew are shift workers and there is an ever changing mix of people working during each shift. Some find it difficult to form stable and lasting working relationships in this context. Personal relationships can suffer too because of long periods away from home. These difficulties can lead to feelings of isolation and loneliness. Accumulated sleep deprivation makes everything feel harder to deal with and can lead to work stress, or physical and emotional ill health.

While it is no surprise to psychologists and human resource professionals, the importance of mental wellbeing in employees of the airline industry isn't discussed in great detail. Air rage, hijacking, bombs on planes, and airline incidents and accidents, as well as the dramatic effects of 11th September 2001, have contributed to anxiety about flight safety among crew and the general public. The importance to crew and their passengers of physical and mental wellbeing cannot be over-stressed. According to media reports covering the crash landing at London Heathrow on 17th of January 2008 of a British Airways flight from Beijing, a potential disaster was avoided largely because of human responses to crisis. The crew onboard the aircraft, despite their own fears, trauma, and anxiety, managed the situation in a professional and calm manner. This, along with extensive training in emergency procedures, ensured the safe evacuation of more than 130 passengers and 15 crew members.

Psychology and aircrew wellbeing

Psychology is a diverse discipline that studies the way people think, feel, and behave. There are many different kinds of psychology and this can often cause confusion for the general public. Some may have already heard of clinical/counselling psychology, occupational/business psychology, social psychology, forensic/criminal psychology or sport psychology to name a few. Mental health professionals use different types of therapy according to his or her preference and speciality as well as the nature of a problem they are treating. Crew who have studied psychology or sought professional help themselves may be aware of these many kinds of therapy which include cognitive-behavioural therapy, psychodynamic therapy, and systemic therapy. This section will focus on a single specialty of psychology that identifies and treats emotional difficulties and stress induced illness.

Like other people, cabin and flight crew may suffer from emotional difficulties at times in their lives. This might be due to relationship difficulties, bereavements, excessive stress, traumatic incidents, or other form of psychological adversity. Most people, including crew can successfully overcome these problems on their own or using the support network around them. Others rely on professionals to help them. Not all people are equally keen on the idea of seeking professional help. Some may worry that sessions with a therapist will clash with their work schedule, particularly if they anticipate weekly support. Most psychologists, counsellors, or psychotherapists are sympathetic towards other peoples' work schedule and can usually offer some flexibility to suit a person's professional life. Crew might be pleasantly surprised by the options available to them and other shift workers. A competent and skilled psychologist, counsellor or psychotherapist can help to identify and deal with the 'root' of problems. There are a number of ways crew can obtain psychological support:

How to obtain psychological support

- Consider scheduling a meeting with your ground based manager to explore what support may be available in your company. It is also in their best interest to provide adequate support to their employees as failure to do so can result in long-term health related absence, reduced work performance, and a high annual staff turnover.
- For those who don't want to speak to their manager, consider enquiring whether there are support systems in the company. Many airlines, especially the larger ones, offer employee support through an occupational health department or a semi-independent employee assistance or counselling service.
- Consider visiting your GP. Many medical practitioners (e.g. a doctor or a nurse) can offer advice on access to appropriate psychological care depending on the problem. They may give you details about counselling services in the local area. Counsellors can help with many problems, including bereavement, anxiety, depression, or drug and alcohol addictions.

- Consider private therapy. Although this approach can be expensive, it might be worth the investment. There are many ways to locate a private therapist. If you live in the UK, you can contact The British Psychological Society (BPS), the British Association for Counselling and Psychotherapy (BACP), or the United Kingdom Council for Psychotherapy (UKCP) who can assist you with finding an accredited therapist.
- Some private medical health insurance schemes cover issues pertaining to one's psychological wellbeing. Seek advice from an insurance representative who can give you further information about private therapy and how to find a suitable therapist.

The stigma attached to mental health problems may prevent some people from seeking professional support. They may feel shame, fear, guilt, or strongly believe that they ought to be able to deal with their 'personal issues' on their own. Long absences away from home may condition crew into high levels of independence and self-reliance. Though psychology is becoming an increasingly accepted and effective way of helping people to deal with emotional difficulties, there are still misconceptions about what it is and what it can offer people.

Case study

John, a cabin crew member, finally decided to seek help from a psychologist after extensive persuasion from his wife who was concerned about his aggressive outbursts following his involvement in a traumatic car accident. He had declined the initial offer of psychological help immediately after the accident. John started his therapy session by telling the psychologist that he was 'not a lunatic', he did not 'believe in psychology', he did not really want to 'attend for a whole year', and that he was certainly 'not going to lie on the couch'. The psychologist explained to John that a lot of people are initially scared of attending therapy because they assume that only those who suffer from serious mental health problems need psychological care. She explained that a majority of her clients are active working individuals who function well despite their problems and that psychology is an advanced form of 'common sense'. It is not a magic cure that one has to believe in or subscribe to. Rather, it encourages and helps people to identify and confront the underlying 'root' of their problems. There is no set time duration for therapy as it will depend upon the specific problem a person is experiencing. Some people may only require a couple of sessions whereas others may benefit from longer term support and she did not have a couch but she had a chair for all of her clients. She explained that the 'couch' was mostly used in the Freudian days when people attended sessions for psychoanalysis. She reassured John that therapy was similar to the conversations that he has at home with his wife. However, unlike his wife, the therapist did not know John and that she hoped he would find it easier to discuss his problems with an objective person. After this discussion, John appeared more relaxed in the session and said that he felt more hopeful about therapy. He continued to attend and together with the help of the therapist, John managed to overcome his angry feelings, which he came to see were triggered by his traumatic experience of the car accident.

Mental health professionals are not confined to the treatment of emotional 'crises'. They are also actively involved in work that aims to prevent emotional illness by offering advice, guidance, and support on how to maintain healthy emotional wellbeing both in the workplace and at home. This includes carrying out research, writing self-help book publications as well as teaching in workshops and educational programmes for the general public. They provide specialist expertise to a number of large organisations including the aviation industry, the media, the National Health Service, as well as a number of large corporate services across the world. They can help deal with crises, redundancies, work stress, and can be drawn in to resolve conflict and enhance management and leadership skills.

Conclusion

The reality of the aircrew lifestyle is far removed from many of the stereotypical views of the profession. Aircrew, like a majority of ground based workers, are earnest people who strive to maintain an adequate work-life balance, look after their emotional wellbeing, and have a high level of work-motivation despite long duty hours and frequent absence from home. To prevent psychological stress and maintain psychological wellness, crew must understand the role they are taking on and appreciate the unique challenges they face. The next chapter details these unique challenges, including the irregular and long work hours, early wake ups, sleep deprivation, jetlag and fatigue. The aim is to increase awareness of the effects of the job on health and to provide tips and guidelines on how to manage the many pressures of a job in the air.

CHAPTER TWO

Jetlag, fatigue and sleep deprivation

Aircrew often work long hours that fall outside of a normal working day. The nature of the job also means that crew are frequently crossing time zones. Not unexpectedly, performance and wellbeing, and an individual's ability to sleep can be affected by these abnormal circumstances. We hear a lot about the effects of jetlag and shift work patterns on performance of aircrew and pilots. This has been taken into account in the development and implementation of flight time limitation regulations, which limit how long pilots can fly, thereby ensuring that their fatigue doesn't jeopardise the safety of the aircraft and passengers. However, we know less about the effects of jetlag and shift working on aircraft crew, not only in terms of their performance, but also how the combined effects of jetlag and shift work affect physical and mental wellbeing both while on duty and upon returning home.

This chapter will discuss the effects of fatigue and sleep deprivation on crews' mental (and to a lesser degree physical) wellbeing. A particular aim is to discuss what causes sleep deprivation and what effects it has on crew's capacity to think, feel, and monitor their performance and behaviour. The chapter also gives general guidance on how to manage fatigue and sleep deprivation.

What is jetlag?

Greenwich Mean Time is a global time standard in which the world is divided into 24 time zones. Time is determined by the distance from the Greenwich Meridian, which passes through London and is the reference point for the system. 15 degrees travel in either direction from this imaginary line will change the time by one hour, with travel to the East adding an hour and travel to the West losing one. When a person crosses over a number of time zones, the body's normal 'circadian' rhythm or 'biological clock' is disrupted. The symptoms of this disruption are collectively known as jetlag. The body clock controls when you are sleepy and alert, as well as your hunger, digestion, bowel habits, urine production, body temperature, and hormone secretion. This internal timekeeper is normally synchronized with your local time so that one feels hungry in the morning and sleepy in the evening. Two of the most important functions of the body clock are in regulating sleep and altering mood and mental performance. Take the example of a crew member travelling from Europe to Africa, i.e. travelling mainly south, compared to someone travelling from Europe to the United States of America (i.e. travelling West). Though the flight times might be quite similar, the journey to Africa won't disrupt the biological clock as much as the journey to the USA. This is largely because the time difference between European time and the United States (–5 to –8h GMT depending on East, Middle, North, or South America) is greater compared to time variations between European and African local time (+1 GMT).

With their own internal clock set to local time, crossing time zones means that crew arrive hours ahead or behind the time they are expecting. Consequently, the body has to adjust to new times of light, darkness, and meals, and often to differences in temperature. It has been suggested that adjusting to new time zones is harder when travelling east (e.g. to Japan, Singapore, Thailand, Vietnam, Australia, New Zealand etc.) because the body finds it more difficult to adjust to a shorter day than to a longer one. This means that it may be easier to delay sleep for a few hours (Westward travel) than to force oneself to fall asleep when one is not ready (Eastward travel). Adjustment to a new time zone can take anything up to ten days depending on age, lifestyle issues, pre-existing physical or mental illness, and the number of time zones crossed within a specific period of travel. A healthy and well rested crew member may adapt more easily to new time zones than someone who is suffering from health related problems or sleep deprivation prior to a trip abroad.

Symptoms of jetlag

Symptoms of jetlag vary from person to person and will depend on the distance travelled and how many time zones are crossed. Common symptoms include:

- Disturbed sleep patterns
- Lack of concentration
- Lack of motivation
- Feeling disorientated, clumsy, or confused
- Decreased mental and physical performance
- Lack of energy
- Headaches
- Irritability
- Loss of appetite
- Disrupted digestion and bowel habits
- Fatigue (extreme tiredness and lack of energy)

The nature of the work means that jetlag is inevitable for aircrew, and it does not become less marked with practice. Aircrew are just as likely to experience disruptions to the body clock as someone who travels less frequently. There are coping mechanisms and techniques that can be learned and used to limit the symptoms of jetlag. The next section introduces some of these.

Before arriving at the destination

- Try to get plenty of sleep in between trips.
- The day before a trip try going to bed and getting up earlier (if travelling East) or later (if travelling West).
- Drink plenty of water on the flight (before and after) as this will help to keep you hydrated.
- Try to eat at the same meal time as your destination. If this does not correspond with service routines onboard the aircraft, a light snack such as fruit or nuts can help crew to slightly adjust their meal patterns.

During the layover period

- Try to allow yourself adequate time to adjust to the new time zone when you arrive. A shower may help you to feel refreshed and can often make one feel more alert. This might ease the process of staying awake if you arrive at a new destination in the day time.
- If possible, get some natural light when you arrive, by having a short walk outside the hotel or in the local surroundings. This will regulate or 'advance' the biological clock.
- Avoid sleep until bedtime; do not nap during the day, as it will not help you adjust to the local time. Though naps might be necessary if crew are required to operate on a late departure for the journey home or additional shuttles to and from the local destination.
- Try to avoid caffeine or alcohol three hours before you go to sleep, as they are stimulants.

- Do not eat a heavy meal before going to sleep (but do not go to bed hungry).
- A relaxing bath can help you feel sleepy and the background sound of the TV or radio may help you sleep. Remember to turn it off before you fall asleep so that the sound does not wake you up during the night.
- Get some exercise everyday, through walking, going to the gym, or doing light stretches/yoga exercises in your room.

Contributing factors

Undeniably, the airline industry is a big business. To maximise revenue, aircraft and cabin crew are required to operate around the clock, working non-standard hours that may be heavy on night shifts and rotating schedules. As in other professions with similar demands—such as industrial shift workers, nurses and doctors, this can exacerbate sleep difficulties and fatigue. The inconsistent and sometimes unpredictable alterations between day and night duties mean that aircrew are required to make rapid adjustments to their changing sleep-cycles. Scheduling and workload often compounds aircrew fatigue.

Fatigue is defined as extreme tiredness and lack of energy. Symptoms include sleepiness and lethargy, cognitive slowness, concentration difficulties and irritability. Short-haul crew often attribute their fatigue to irregular sleep patterns and a heavy workload. Both long-haul and short-haul aviation workers commonly attribute their fatigue with night flights, jetlag, early wakeups, time pressure, multiple flight legs, and consecutive duty periods without time to recover in between. For long-haul crew members there are in-flight sleep opportunities, usually of 2 to 4 hours duration. These are scheduled only during the cruise segment of the flight and often in-between meal services since this is a time of low work loads for both the pilots and the cabin crew. Although the anticipation of a 'break' away from the cockpit or in-flight service routines can have a positive effect on motivation and mood and sleep during a shift can help to keep you alert and performing optimally, the reality can be somewhat different. Noise, turbulence, temperature, lighting, and other comfort factors mean that sleep, even when there is a space to do it, isn't always possible.

Hours of work

Long-haul

A typical long-haul aircrew schedule involves a monthly plan of up to five worldwide trips. Duty days vary in length between 11 and 16 hours depending on the destination in question. Although most outbound flights leave during the morning or afternoon, return flights tend to depart late in the evening or during the night. As well as the fatigue associated with a long overnight shift mood and performance will be poorer at night, because the sleep-wake schedule is out of synchrony with the body clock. Some crew remain awake for longer than the usual 16 hours if their flight does not leave until the evening and they have been awake all day.

Layovers vary in length too, from less than 24 hours to several days. Ideally, the time should be used to rest and recuperate from the effects of the outward flight in preparation for the return of the journey. Sometimes crew have the problem of deciding whether or not to try and adjust their sleep-wake cycle and body clock to the new time zone. Surveys of long-haul crew of major UK airlines have shown that this is a very real concern. On international flights, the rest periods in between trips will vary according to number of time zones crossed, the total length of the trip, and duty hours onboard the aircraft. For example, a 5 day duty trip from Europe to the Far East may allow crew up to 4 days rest before their next duty period. In contrast, a similar length trip to Africa may only permit for 2 days at home due to shorter flight times and less time zone changes.

The amount of time crew have to rest between their departures and the balance of their day and night shifts contribute to feelings of fatigue, and the crew agreed that there were two approaches to managing jetlag. The first was to make an effort to adjust to the local time, while the second was to try to remain on European time. Adjusting to the local time allows individuals to engage with local facilities on longer trips and to sleep during hours of darkness. However, remaining on European time is believed to ease the process of readjustment to the time back home once crew returned. If the individual has been successful in attempts to stay on home time when away from home, then readjustment of the sleep wake cycle and the body clock should not be required once he or she has returned. However, if he or she attempted to adjust to destination time, then the process of adjustment back to home time must be accomplished after arrival home.

Short-haul

On short-haul operations, crew are usually required to work about six consecutive duty days. These can range from single to double return trips per day, domestic or European stopovers (non-European airlines may operate short flights to nearby countries such as Singapore-Malaysia), or a combination of both. Short-haul crew aren't as likely as those doing longer flights to suffer the effects of many time zone transitions but early wake ups and late finishes are a feature of their work. Early starts for morning flights may interrupt a night's sleep. For example, a typical duty day for a London based airline may involve a 5.30 am start for a return flight to Paris followed by a return trip to Rome that arrives back late in the evening. The next day may involve an early flight to Glasgow and back again followed by a short layover in Oslo. A similar schedule may be repeated for the entire work period before the crew can enjoy a well-earned rest period, typically of about 3 days. Short-haul crew may have heavier workloads and more frequent early wakeups while long-haul commercial aircrew are experiencing sleep difficulties because of disruptions to their body clocks.

Cumulative sleep deprivation

Repeated travel to different time zones and/or consecutive early starts and late finishes can lead to cumulative sleep deprivation. This is intensified if crew don't get enough rest between trips. The effects of cumulative sleep deprivation include cognitive, emotional, somatic, and behavioural changes. 'Cognition' refers to processes in the brain that enable activities such as thinking, learning and judgment.

Effects of cumulative sleep deprivation

Cognitive
- Memory loss, impaired performance, speech problems, disorientation, inability to 'think straight', irrational thought processes.

Emotional
- Irritability, annoyance, feeling grouchy, weepy, feeling sensitive, sadness.

Physical
- Lethargy, loss of energy, loss of motivation, digestive problems, cold and flu symptoms, headaches.

Behavioural
- 'Odd presentation' (may say things to others that does not make sense), irrational actions (may drive at excessive speed on the motorway because it 'seems' like a good idea to get home 'quicker'), carelessness (dropping objects, spilling fluids, leaving personal belongings behind)

The symptoms resemble the inevitable tiredness that follows a night flight or a long duty day, and it may be difficult for crew, and others, to notice the negative changes. Impaired performance can challenge a person's sense of competence, and others may mistake concentration difficulties for 'dumbness', or irritability for 'being rude'. When surveyed, UK aircrew acknowledged that prolonged periods of sleep deprivation often disrupted their emotions and cognition. These effects were not always short lived. The inability to identify such disruptions may lead to serious consequences, both for the individual crew member and for the safety of the aircraft. Some of you, particularly those with extensive flying experience will recognise the effects that cognitive disruption caused by sleep deprivation can have on mental wellbeing.

This may help you recognise the symptoms of fatigue

- Can you remember a time when you have felt fatigued for more than two weeks?
- If you are unable to do so try and think about the immediate tiredness that can sometime arise from flying through the night/or an early wake up?
- Did you notice any emotional, cognitive, or behavioural changes in yourself? For example, did you find it difficult to motivate yourself?
- Fatigue affects people in different ways, so it is important that you try to identify how fatigue affects **you.** For example, a person who is prone to irritability or tearfulness may experience these symptoms on a regular basis regardless of fatigue.
- A good way of separating symptoms of fatigue from your individual characteristics may be to ask yourself 'how would I normally deal with this situation?', 'am I usually this grouchy towards my partner?' Honesty is a key factor here as it is easy to 'blame' negative behaviours on 'jetlag' (this can be very tempting after an argument with loved ones in the hopes that they will let you off the hook!)

Generally, crew can prevent over tiredness by getting adequate sleep. The problems come when the effects build up and it becomes difficult to recognise the severity of your symptoms and harder to implement strategies to overcome fatigue. Work shifts and short periods of rest in-between trips may prevent crew from catching up on all the sleep they need. To honour their contracts, all employees must turn up for work. For aircrew, the reality is a requirement to operate even with clear symptoms of sleep deprivation and fatigue. Aircrew pay scales vary between airlines, though a substantial portion is usually made up of overseas allowances. These are not granted unless the individual reports for work, so financial commitments (mortgage or other regular payments), may complicate the act of admitting fatigue.

Cognition and fatigue

In simple terms, the human cognitive processing system (e.g. your cognition) is largely responsible for regulating the way you 'think', make decisions, solve problems, perceive a situation, remember information, and carry out tasks. It is also related to language, emotions, and social interactions. These complex processes occur in the brain which is why cognition is often associated with terms such as 'mental powers', 'braininess' or 'intellectual ability'. For crew and pilots in particular, perception, memory, and concentration are important. In all people, the performance of these functions are limited and you can not see, hear, or pay attention to everything that is happening in the environment all at once. A control centre in the brain juggles these processes, deciding what to give resources to in a way that depends on the external environment, what tasks are in hand, or arising emergencies. This control centre is very important to every day activities, at home and during work as it allows you to balance various obligations, learn new tasks, respond to dangerous situations (e.g. a fire), keep conversations flowing, run, and eat and so on.

Learning new tasks may require more attention than performing those that have become part of daily routines such as driving a car, making a cup of tea or other everyday activities. As tasks become more and more familiar with practice, they tend to become 'automatic' and require less input from the cognitive control centres in the brain. Most people can perform more than one task at a time, and the more skilled a person is at those tasks, the easier it is to 'multitask' them. For example, it may be easier for a skilled driver to hold a conversation while driving than it is for someone who is still learning. There are limits to people's capacity for 'dual tasking' even if two or more exercises are considered to be highly automated as in the case of reading a book while also trying to watch TV. Both reading and watching TV require visual attention to relay information to the brain to be processed. When two or more tasks, automatic or not, rely on the same 'input channel' for receiving information, performance can be disrupted.

Every day we face difficulties in multi-tasking with certain activities. Consider these:

- Have you ever tried to hold a conversation while at the same time mentally planning tomorrow's event out with friends?
- Did you come away from the conversation realising that you had no idea what the other person said or that you could not remember a single topic of the discussion?
- These difficulties are common and do not indicate problems with memory. Instead, you were distracted by thoughts of the next day's plans, and because it is difficult to concentrate closely on two things at the same time, some details of the conversation may have gone unregistered, e.g. they didn't even make it into your memory.

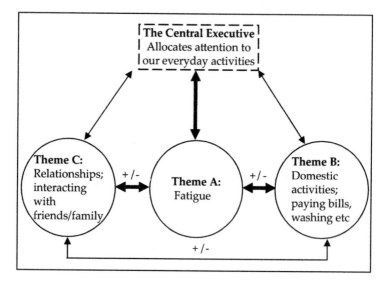

Diagram 1. The interactions between everyday activities and their connection to the higher level 'control centre' (Eriksen, 2006).

Cognition is a complex set of processes about which many books have been written. The illustration below simplifies the relationship between excessive fatigue and mental capacity.

Theme A in the diagram above represents fatigue caused by repeated experiences of sleep loss whereas theme B and C represent activities that people are engaged in on an everyday basis. The width of the arrows between the centres of cognitive control (the central executive) and the themes (A, B, and C) illustrates how much of a demand that theme puts on cognitive processing. In the case of aircrew, fatigue that results from cumulative sleep deprivation reduces a person's functional memory, their capacity to pay attention, and how they perceive things. In other words, their entire cognitive repertoire is known to suffer. When demands are high, the central processor must decide how to allocate its resources.

In the case of aircrew, fatigue means the processor tries to compensate by allocating the majority of its resources to restoring capacities for memory, concentration, and perception. This is illustrated by the thick arrow between theme A and the central executive in the above diagram. Unfortunately, this also means that there is little capacity left for the completion of other tasks such as dealing with relationships (theme C) or carrying out domestic activities (theme B). This imbalance is illustrated by the thinner arrows between task B and C and the central executive in the diagram above. The diagram is only illustrative and doesn't mean that fatigued crew are incapable of interacting with others or completing domestic duties. Instead, it shows how fatigue places heavy demands on cognition, interfering with a person's 'normal' performance, presentation, or way of being. Sleep deprived crew who arrive back home after a long flight during the night may find domestic responsibilities such as laundry or paying bills more strenuous and time consuming than usual. Likewise, interactions with others, whether a colleague, a family member or a friend, may feel as if it requires more energy, concentration, or patience than when a crew member is fully rested and alert.

Case study

Janet, a long-haul cabin crew member, visited a psychologist for help with reduced motivation, clumsiness, and difficulties with completing her daily chores including cleaning, paying bills and grocery shopping. She described her problems as 'lying awake until the early hours of the morning' and would often feel tired and 'exhausted' the following day. Janet strongly believed that her sleep pattern was 'messed up' because of work. On the other hand, she also explained that she had been a 'bad sleeper' prior to starting her job as cabin crew. Janet's problem appeared to stem from a feeling of excessive pressure to fall asleep at night. She said she 'dreaded' feeling tired the next morning as this would often result in grouchiness, feeling sensitive, and 'completely useless'. At night time, Janet would often lie in bed and worry about 'not falling asleep'. This, in turn, caused her to 'tense up' and feel anxious, which made it even harder for Janet to drift off. Thus, Janet's strong beliefs about the catastrophic consequences surrounding sleep deprivation created extra pressures of sleep that made it more difficult for her to establish a healthy sleep pattern.

Fatigue also affects decision making, making it harder to reach sensible verdicts when presented with competing choices. On a simple level it may affect the ability to weigh up the potential positive and negative consequences of a choice. More dramatically, it may affect ability to make the rapid decisions that are required during catastrophic situations such as an aircraft emergency, fire in the layover hotel, or in situations where personal safety is being threatened. Predicting exactly how you or the people around you will respond in the time of a crisis is impossible because everyone has a different anxiety threshold. As these thresholds are affected by lack of sleep, work routines and flight schedules should be sensitive to this and pilots and cabin crew should learn to recognise when their bodies are fatigued.

Fatigue in daily life

The only cure for fatigue is adequate sleep. Aircrew can improve their sleep habits through relaxation therapy, which they can do themselves, and by avoiding heavy exercise and caffeine before bed. It sounds easy, but family and other relationship demands are an added pressure. Not unexpectedly, the added pressure of one's unique work requirements, particularly long periods away from family or a partner add stress to relationships, to a degree that might be more than that experienced by other shift workers or the general population. This stress, in turn, affects sleep patterns.

There are many demands competing for space in the life of an aircrew member. The need for adequate sleep must often compete with the need to service relationships with family, friends and a partner. The precise effects on physical and mental wellbeing vary according to an individual's personal characteristics and the circumstances in which they must manage their stress. For example, a married female with children might use her time away from home to recuperate from the strains of looking after two young toddlers. By prioritising, for example, sleep instead of socialising with colleagues during the layover period, a fully rested mother may not feel she needs to sleep as soon as she returns. This, in turn, allows her more time for her family. In contrast, crew members who continuously sacrifice sleep for social or independent activities, both at home and during the layover period are likely to suffer more from the negative effects of fatigue. Although going out with friends or spending time with a partner can, in the short-term, reduce the immediate stress arising from fears of neglecting ones personal relationships, the longer term effect of continuously favouring 'others' above one's own need for sleep can seriously affect cognitive health and emotions.

Case study

Mark, a short haul commercial airline pilot, sought help from a counsellor for his concentration difficulties, mood 'swings', and lack of energy. He described the cause of his difficulties as 'never having a moment to himself' because of work and family commitments. Mark clearly believed that he had to 'make' the most out of his time with family and friends at home and that he should always 'agree' to go out for a drink with colleagues when away. He strongly believed in socialising having witnessed his parent's failure to engage in social events or inviting visitors to their home. He was therefore determined to ensure he did not 'become' as 'lonely' and 'boring' as his parents. Consequently, Mark spent very little time resting before and in-between trips. His previous experiences and the beliefs which arose from them made it difficult for him to balance his need to relax and sleep with the many opportunities to socialise both at work and at home.

There are techniques that can be used to manage jetlag and fatigue. UK based aircrew admit that learning them is a gradual process, requiring practical experience of long trips, of managing large time differences and of dealing with the strain of flying through the night. The effects of jetlag and fatigue are dependent upon who's experiencing them, and so too are the ways that they are managed. Experience of your own response to time change will determine whether you try to adjust to local times. Some may choose to stay on UK time, feeling that having to readjust when they get back home is wasted time that could be better spent with loved ones. This must be weighed up against the consequences of choosing to stay on UK time while in a foreign place. It might be harder to engage with colleagues or to take advantage of local facilities if you need to sleep when others are away. During longer trips this might increase feelings of loneliness and isolation. These decisions are personal ones that aircrew make as they adjust to the way their body responds to working conditions.

A period of readjustment is often needed when returning home. When interviewed, crew said that how this was managed depended on what time of day they arrived back home. Sleeping for a couple of hours if arriving home before 1400 local time was a common strategy felt to help ease crew back into a more regular sleep pattern. However, crew had to try not to over-sleep which might result in them being nocturnal for a majority of the period of time spent at home. If they arrived later than 1400 hours the interviewees' said they would often try and stay awake during the day and then have an early night. They all confirmed that sleep deprivation and fatigue affected their health and performance in a whole range of issues including psychological and physical wellbeing, and their ability maintain professional, social, and intimate relationships.

There are other ways to deal with jetlag and tiredness, many of which are linked to relaxation and preparing your body for sleep. Regular exercise for example, or reading, listening to calm music or using herbal and other remedies to aid sleep (though this was controversial) were common approaches. There is no guarantee that any of these strategies work, and some crew spoke about extended periods without sleep (up to 24 hours) despite their best efforts.

Recommendations for fatigue prevention

- Get as much sleep as possible to prevent fatigue and keep your mind and emotions healthy.
- Don't be pre-occupied with your sleep pattern. If you can't fall asleep after 20 to 30 minutes in bed get up and do something to distract yourself from trying.
- Learn what your body needs and make sensible sleep decisions. Regular naps can help you adjust to a new time zone, but you can oversleep too.
- Think ahead. Manage your layover time in a way that complements the pressures of your home life when you return. Use the time to sleep if you know you'll be busy when you get back.
- Listen to your body and be kind to yourself. This might involve learning to decline invitations for social engagements or saying no to friends, family or colleagues when one is too tired to participate in activities.
- Treat yourself to a massage, aromatherapy oils or other forms of holistic treatments as these can serve to reenergize your mental and physical being.

- Don't neglect your diet as healthy eating can increase energy levels, help the digestion system, and enhance positive mood.

Conclusion

Unusual work schedules, as are common in the airline industry, can disrupt sleep patterns leading to sleep deprivation and fatigue. The only real cure for fatigue is adequate sleep. However, the simultaneous pressure of domestic duties and home demands may mean that getting enough sleep is not easy. Cumulative sleep deprivation can lead to more serious consequences, with individuals becoming increasingly irrational, de-motivated, exhausted, and moody. A healthy balance of social living and sleep management can help crew deal better with the impact of work requirements on their sleep hygiene. Sleep is not the only pressure for air crew. As the complements of staff on board often change for each flight, the brief and short lasting relationships at work can be an added strain. The dynamics between aircrew, both onboard the aircraft and during the layover period, is the focus of the next chapter. There we try to paint a realistic picture of social interactions between colleagues who must rely upon each other in quite unique circumstances while spending time away from home. The discussions about group dynamics will give you greater appreciation for the different ways people behave and will help you to think about how to manage conflicts at work if they arise.

CHAPTER THREE

Professional relationships

As is the case with all employees, good working relationships are important for productivity and job satisfaction. Aircrew face a set of unique challenges when it comes to forming relationships with their work colleagues. Each time they start a new duty trip, crew are likely to be travelling with a different set of people. Reporting for work each day usually includes meeting colleagues for the first time. When the trip is over crew members say their farewells and there is no guarantee that they will ever work with each other again. First impressions can be lasting and they often shape, for better or for worse, the nature of the group dynamics onboard an aircraft. This set up provides limited opportunities to develop stable and long lasting relationships through the work environment. Though for some people, travelling with new colleagues is an ideal opportunity to engage with a variety of different personalities, for others, working each time with a group of 'strangers' can be difficult. This chapter attempts to provide a realistic account of professional relationships as experienced by crew themselves.

Group dynamics

The success of the airline industry is built around functioning teams. Crew are usually recruited because of their positive characteristics which should ease their ability to relate to others. The exact criteria required depend upon the airline in question, but characteristics such as flexibility, openness, empathy, and friendliness are undeniably important. They reflect an individual's ability to work with others and to communicate effectively both of which are crucial aspects of the job. From an organisational point of view, crew are expected to operate in a professional and effective manner. Emergency routines, such as an aircraft evacuation or responding to a fire or a medical incident, rely heavily on people working together. Different airlines adopt different emergency procedures, but the standard CAA (Civil Aviation Authority) requires the joint skills and communication of a minimum of 3 to 4 individuals to effect rapid aircraft evacuations. In line with this huge responsibility, there is a tremendous pressure on crew members to work as a group that is strong enough to deal effectively with any issues that may arise onboard the aircraft. The requirement to reform this group for each flight is a real additional pressure.

As discussed in chapter 1, crew usually attend a 20 minute briefing before passengers board the aircraft. The primary purpose of this is to allocate working positions and to ensure appropriate commercial and safety awareness. The briefing is often the first time crew get to meet their colleagues and their capacity to develop a strong working alliance with each other depends upon a host of factors, including:

- the personalities of each individual within the team
- the style in which they are managed by the chief cabin crew member and the captain in command
- extent of sleep deprivation and fatigue (which can affect interactional skills and motivation)

- adverse environmental conditions may affect behaviour (e.g. lack of oxygen and poor air-circulation)

These difficulties will be familiar to those who have been involved in the profession for any length of time. The routine of 'getting to know' up to 18 new people per shift (on long-haul flights) can be emotionally exhausting. It is sometimes tempting to put aside your own needs in order to project the most attractive side of your personality. Establishing a rapport with colleagues may be easy on one trip and hard work on the next. This isn't always because of individual differences between the people onboard. Sometimes the pressures of everyone striving towards effective individual and group relationships can take its toll. Some might end up resenting their colleagues or their profession, feeling they are part of a superficial workforce with little or no 'genuine' interactions. For more sensitive people, there may be serious consequences of these feelings.

These challenges can be addressed through trying to maintain a positive environment at work. Techniques to achieve this include active listening, expressing openness toward the group/colleagues, discussing shared topics of interest, and using humour to promote a pleasant working environment. Repeating personal anecdotes and 'standard crew questioning' are two ways of helping people feel included.

Group conflict

The majority of flights proceed without major conflicts amongst the crew. However, different factors affect the level at which people have bonded and therefore the team dynamics. When problems arise there is the additional challenge of finding a way to manage these in the confined space onboard. This is especially relevant for pilots who are usually expected to remain on the flight deck for the duration of the flight. For cabin crew, who on longer journeys are typically divided into 2 to 4 different teams, it may be easier to manage conflict or to maximise group functioning by arranging team members sensitively. Crew with more experience of flying soon come to learn that the relationships don't last long and may be better at a *'grin and bear it'* strategy.

Case study

Angela, a senior first officer for a commercial airline was working with a male captain who had recently separated from his wife. Angela was due to marry her long-term partner at the end of the month and was telling the Captain about her 'big day'. During the conversation she noticed that the Captain would often interrupt her and that he was very quick to highlight the negative sides of marriage, love, and partnerships. Although Angela found the Captain's remarks both upsetting and annoying, she knew that she only 'had to put up with him' for a few more hours. She changed the subject and avoided taking his comments to heart. Angela's experience of the short-lasting relationships with her colleagues helped her to initiate positive actions and to avert a potential conflict between her and the Captain. The initiative to change topic of conversation helped her to remain positive, professional, and courteous towards the Captain for the remainder of the flight.

Conflict can negatively affect attempts to socialise during the layover period. Crew who are faced with such situations may experience long periods of isolation, loneliness and boredom. They may question their social abilities when they're not getting on with colleagues and this can heighten their self-doubt and feelings of being unpopular or disliked. There is a simple method used by many psychologists to encourage positive thinking during periods of conflict. This is simply to ask yourself whether it is realistic for you to expect to 'get on' with each of the many hundreds of individuals you work with every year.

People attach different meanings to experiences, leading to an array of different emotional (healthy or unhealthy feelings) and behavioural (constructive or destructive actions) responses to one situation. The idea that 'people feel the way they think' is a central tenet of Cognitive Behavioural Therapy (CBT). CBT is growing in popularity as an effective treatment with long-term benefits for many different psychological problems. It is based on the principle that people can live more happily and productively if they are thinking in healthy ways. Unhealthy thoughts have negative effects on emotions, behaviours and motivations. For example, consider a situation where two differing cabin crew members (Person A and Person B) are both part of a six crew team working in the world traveller cabin. Throughout the flight there have been conflicts with other crew members. The resulting atmosphere is difficult with little or no communication between individuals. The diagram below illustrates two possible interpretations of the situation on board by the two different crew members.

Healthy versus unhealthy thinking in conflict situations

Person A: 'I should have tried harder to 'get on' with the crew', 'It's all my fault', 'Nobody likes me'

The effects of person A's thinking: **Emotional** (depressed, lonely), **Behavioural** (calls in sick for work, avoids seeing friends, watches TV all day), **Motivational** (does not want to see other people or engage in activities)

> Person B: 'It's a different combination of personalities on each flight—it is not going to work each time'
>
> ↓
>
> The effects of person B's thinking: **Emotional** (sad but not depressed), **Behavioural** (sleeps well, engages with friends/ family at home), **Motivational** (feels ready to go to work again)

Some emotional responses are healthier than others. There are 'healthy' negative emotions and feeling bad when bad things happen is natural. However, unhealthy negative emotions make situations seem worse. For example, feeling sad (a healthy negative emotion) is less serious than feeling intensely depressed (an unhealthy negative emotion). Feeling sadness may prompt people to improve their situation, e.g. by seeing friends and family, but depression is more likely to lead people to inaction and resignation including withdrawal from friends and activities.

As person B was able to do, increased experience of the realities of forever changing crew composition may encourage this acceptance of the fact that perfect relationships with all colleagues at all times is impossible. UK based long-haul workers make a distinction between 'good' and 'bad' crew based on this.

Dealing with group conflict

> • Conflict and disagreements happen at work; they needn't be a problem. In a conflict situation use your negotiation skills, be open to different viewpoints, listen and show good will. These qualities help keep discussions moving until a resolution can be found.

- Be sensible about the way you relate to your colleagues. A smile and positive body language are effective ways to prevent a negative atmosphere onboard the aircraft.
- Speak to a colleague or supervisor if you are finding it hard to control your emotions, particularly if your difficulties are related to personal circumstances. People will be more sympathetic and will more readily empathise and offer support if they know what's going on.
- Be sensitive to the fact that your colleagues might be having their own personal problems. Inconstant moods are a clue that this could be the case.
- Finally, ask yourself whether it is worth getting involved in a conflict. Controlled conflict can be constructive, e.g. to deal with people who cause problems, but be sensible and sensitive and follow appropriate guidelines (e.g. inform your supervisor who can bring the topic to the attention of the respective person).

Personal belonging

Crew spend a considerable amount of their time away from home. On longer routes, trips can last from 3 to 12 days. During this time, individuals are away from what is familiar to them and must join a group of strangers. A positive working relationship with these people can provide a supportive substitute network for crew who have left behind families and friends. However, the brief nature of crew relations may interfere with the ability to form meaningful, non-superficial relationships and can increase feelings of isolation and loneliness.

UK airline crew agree that the level of social engagement during the layover period is very closely linked to the first impressions of their colleagues. There are greater opportunities to form relationships with colleagues who are perceived to be friendly, communicative, or outgoing. Transforming superficial encounters into something more meaningful improves a positive sense of self and adds value to any trip. By bearing a resemblance to out-of-work friendships, having closer one to one relationships with colleagues can ease feelings of isolation. Establishing an alliance with a colleague can limit the amount of time spent alone and reduce the risk of boredom and loneliness. Interactions during layovers may also encourage more personal working relationships and improve team functioning upon return to the aircraft.

There are different kinds of relationships and for some there is little or no choice about whether to stay in it or not. For example, a child does not choose his or her parents and there are strong prohibitions against a person totally rejecting other family members. At work, there are many situations where people are more or less 'forced' (if they want to keep their jobs) to enter into relationships with people they might not otherwise choose to spend much time with. 'Closed' situations such as working onboard an aircraft 'throw' people together and may encourage less formal engagements with people. However, the transition from 'casual' to 'close' relationships requires more than just physical proximity. To an extent, crew can regulate the degree of closeness (or distance) when considering their relationships at work and there is potential for people to select from the group the ones they wish to 'befriend'. Within a flight there may be several opportunities to initiate new relationships. Particular crew members may have similarities with one another that ease the formation of a 'friendship'. For example, crew with families may have a considerable amount in common with each other. Likewise, those who are interested in fitness may decide to attend a gym session together.

Outside of work, engaging in group activities such as sightseeing, or going to bars or restaurants are ways to get to know colleagues. It is important to remember that group interaction is not of equal value to each member of a group. The group dynamic and individual desires and preferences guide how important this is to each crew member. The size of the group can determine the type of interactions between individual members. In larger groups, topics of conversation typically centre on general subjects such as work or current affairs. For more confident crew members, such a group size presents an opportunity to engage in lively debates, share one's views, or to demonstrate leadership skills by directing conversations. Those without such social confidence may feel validated or more accepted by simply being a part of such a gathering. Large crew gatherings can often bear the transient characteristics that are seen onboard the aircraft. A gathering such as this may limit the opportunity for individuals to exchange more personal information: crew agree on a time to meet in the hotel lobby, proceed to the point of social activity, engage in the activity, and then make their way back to the hotel. Many may feel like strangers even when they are part of the group, and this can trigger a number of negative emotions including loneliness, discomfort, and homesickness.

Meeting up in smaller groups, e.g. with one or two colleagues at the time, can improve the sense that the interactions have some substance. Smaller groups also give less confident people a chance to bypass some of the awkwardness and strangeness associated with larger gatherings. Intimacy can be built between people by sharing personal details or mutual interests. Intimacy means different things for different people, some feeling that playing sport together for example is an intimate engagement, while for others it means being able to discuss apparently trivial topics easily. Others may feel a need to share details and discuss intimate details of their lives. In interviews, UK based aircrew described how many of their colleagues, including themselves, openly shared personal information with other crew even though they had not known them for more than a couple of hours, or at the most a couple of days. They believed that this allowed them a brief sensation of security and being at ease with colleagues, and was likely to be a mechanism to compensate for the constantly changing crew compositions. Some crew explained how the act of getting to know one's colleagues can become repetitive, increasing emotional tiredness. The apparent routine of asking and being asked the same questions such as *'where do you live?'*, *'have you got a boyfriend/girlfriend?'*, *'what does he/she do for a living?* was thought to be tedious and superficial to some. The shallow nature of professional relationships is seen as a major disadvantage of the job, and many crew express desire for systems that allow them to travel with the same set of colleagues on a more permanent basis. They believed this would increase stability and continuity at work.

Independent functioning

Socialising during a trip is obviously not dependent entirely upon group dynamics. Some people may choose to spend time by themselves, especially if they have a busy social life at home. For some, going away provides a break from childcare, studies, domestic duties, and could be an ideal time to catch up on lost sleep. However, not all people have the same capacity for independent functioning and some may feel anxious about having to spend too much time by themselves. If this is the case for you, use the hotel gym, see some sights, go shopping or have a walk in the local surroundings. With practice you may become more independent or reinforce your natural inclination for independent functioning.

Conclusion

Each time they report for a duty trip, aircrew must engage in a fast paced process of 'forming and breaking' relationships. The opportunities to develop stable and supportive work relationships with people are very limited. For some, this is emotionally tiring and can increase the sense of alienation and isolation both at work and at home. Feeling that work and home relationships are under strain can threaten crew's psychological wellbeing.

Firstly, failures to sustain both social and work relations can lead an individual to feel increasingly lonely and depressed. This may occur when a crew member is predominately alone during layover periods, which is then followed by very few, if any, social encounters at home. Secondly, a supportive network of significant others, whether at home or at work, can help an individual to better deal with everyday challenges. This includes disruptive passengers, financial worries, physical illness or any other situations pertaining to a crew member's personal life. Whereas the present chapter is concerned with professional relationships at work, the next chapter will focus on aircrews' social relationships at home. The nature of a social network varies from one individual to another, though specific features of the aircrew work schedule are thought to challenge crew's ability to develop and maintain social relationships.

CHAPTER FOUR

Social relationships

Considering the irregular hours that aircrew keep and their frequent absences from home, it is not surprising that friendships are put under some degree of strain. Crew may find it hard to commit to social events because they haven't much control over their work schedule and can't plan ahead. Missing out on important engagements including birthday parties, weddings, and family gatherings is part and parcel of the life of an aircrew member. It helps to keep in regular contact with people through telephone calls or emails. The pressure of trying to fit everyone in sometimes means that the period in-between trips can become a catch up period where one is trying to keep up to date with domestic tasks, attend social gatherings that may have been rearranged to coincide with leave and to get some sleep. To juggle these demands and successfully combine a social life with the unavoidably erratic work patterns, individuals must draw on their own organisational skills. It helps to also have an awareness of systems offered by the employer that may help to maintain a work-life balance. In this chapter we will discuss the challenges that crew face when they try to combine a healthy social calendar with the demands of their job. Several factors affect how these pressures are managed and these are discussed in turn.

Low work control

Typically, aircrew receive a monthly schedule of work from their employers. This details the departure dates, times, and durations of duty flights and the number of days allocated between them. Long-haul crew will usually do about 5 overseas trips per month. Short-haul crew will have more frequent trips of shorter duration. Once the schedule is set, there is little room for negotiation. Current systems are not very flexible, and making last minute changes or alterations to scheduled trips may be difficult. Some employers have introduced processes to improve individual control, e.g. a 'bidding' system where crew can 'bid' for the trips they prefer. This strategy can improve a sense of work control and may make it easier for crew to fit in existing social engagements, or other appointments.

Crew often spend up to 20 days per month away from home. Such lengthy absences obviously put pressure on social relationships. The glamour associated with global travel is often accompanied with disappointment, frustration and worry. Not unlike employees in other industries, work responsibilities can take over personal lives. After joining the airline industry, new crew members may notice how acute these feelings are. Where they can, it is important to actively try to regain control of the situation. Airlines vary in the degree to which they facilitate and are sympathetic to the work-life balance of their employees. Most are, either by law or pressure from work unions, required to offer some degree of flexibility. Major airlines may allow their crew to use their leave selectively by applying for specific days off.

These are never guaranteed though and depend on whether the airline can spare the staff. A strategy such as this gives crew a better sense of control over their job schedule and what effects their work is having on social engagements and relationships. Crew must come to understand the formalities and requirements of the airline they work for and fit in to its culture. Failure to be proactive when managing your social life means you might miss out on important engagement, which in turn can have a tremendous impact on close relationships.

It isn't easy to learn how to achieve harmony between competing pressures and this can sometimes be a complex, lengthy process. Here are some suggestions that should help when dealing with irregular patterns of work:

- Familiarise yourself with your employer's guidelines around taking leave.
- Be particularly aware of the notice period you need to give to book leave. Some airlines require applications up to three months in advance whereas other employers are more flexible.
- Be proactive by educating friends and family about the system you work in. This will encourage the people around you to give you sufficient warning about upcoming events.
- If you are unable to achieve the requested day off from work you may wish to contact your manager to see if there are any other options available. It might be worth noting that the degree of support obtained from a manager may depend upon the reasoning of your request. For example, a manger may be more willing to help if the matter is deemed important (e.g. medical appointment) than if you were just planning a regular night out with friends.

- Use the request system even if there aren't specific days you need to take off. Regular down time during your work schedule will be good for your sleep hygiene and may make planning social events easier.

A balance between work and life has a different meaning for each individual. Some will find it easier than others to manage the pressures that work puts on relationships. People who feel they are not managing to achieve this balance may suffer. In interviews, crew were very aware of the negative effects that excessive worrying about this could have on their mental health. It is not always easy to have control over your thinking patterns, particularly when, like crew, there can be long stretches of time if not alone then certainly away from people who are familiar. Low mood, tearfulness, and anxiety are not uncommon, and tiredness can make it harder to deal with these feelings. Fatigue can have a real negative impact making everything seem more difficult. Crew who are fatigued may suffer more than they would if they were fully rested and alert. Unfortunately, the problems can be cyclic, with lack of sleep compounding negative emotions and negative emotions, such as worry and anxiety disrupting sleep further. To unpick these emotional complexities, try asking yourself the following questions;

- Why am I feeling upset?
- Could I have over-reacted because I'm tired?
- Does it help me to worry about the problem?
- Can I talk to anyone on the crew about my worries?
- Are there some activities I can engage in to distract me from these feelings?
- Will a telephone call to a friend at home help cheer me up a bit?
- How long have I had this problem?
- Is it worth seeking professional advice at home to help me cope better with the problem?

Staying positive

All jobs have their positive and negative aspects. The lifestyle offered by the airline industry retains its appeal and is still considered one of the most 'glamorous ways of life'. Many thousands of crew around the world are being paid to fulfil their own and many other people's dream of travelling the world. In the face of unique challenges presented by the job it can be difficult to stay positive. Weighing up the pros and cons of your profession, typically by making comparison with other industries, is a good way to highlight the key differences. Cheap air travel is a perk of the job for crew and their families and friends. Aircrew may be able to treat their partner, friends, or family to holidays that otherwise may be too costly to consider. The contrasts between regular 9-5 office work and the crew lifestyle, in particular the distinct hours of work, routine versus irregularity, consistent place of work versus diverse work environments, same colleagues versus constant changes to the workforce, stuck in front of the computer versus sunbathing on a beach in Australia, may allow individuals to develop a more comprehensive view of their particular type of work. This, in turn, can buffer negative work experiences, and put instances of frustration and disappointment in context. No matter how difficult or stressful a particular profession is, it is important to identify the ways in which, at least to a degree, workers have a choice; they can get 'miserable' about their jobs or they can accept the realities of the particular lifestyle they have chosen to pursue.

Over time, crew will accumulate a range of diverse experiences of the profession, and develop skills that allow them to adjust to new challenges. Familiarity with the pressures at work will help them to have more realistic expectations of the impacts of work on their personal lives. A rational and balanced approach will help to buffer the inevitable disappointments that accompany conflicts with social calendars. Socialising with colleagues during the layover period is a good way to stay positive. This helps to keep one's thoughts off home. It can also be a great stress reliever to relax in company.

Nurturing social relationships

The extent to which friends and family are sympathetic towards work requirements has an effect on how easy it is to achieve a balance between work and home life. It can only be helpful to be surrounded by supportive friends or family who understand the pressures and have realistic expectations of what level of commitment is possible. Consider this scenario:

- Think about having to tell someone that you could not attend their wedding, birthday party or a christening etc.
- What would your initial feelings be when telling them? Would you feel anxious? Would you feel guilty?
- How would they react? Would they be angry, disappointed or sympathetic?
- How would their reaction in turn make you feel? Would you be relieved by their response? Surprised? More or less guilty? Upset?

One way to reduce the risks of disappointment in others is to teach them about the realities of the profession. Regular and open communication about possible interruptions to upcoming social arrangements as well as just keeping in regular contact is very important.

I can't do … . but I can do …

- Call or email friends to maintain contact even if you can't see them during the period of days that you are off from work.
- Remember and acknowledge important occasions for the people around you even if you can't attend the celebrations.
- Suggest more suitable alternatives if you have to turn down a meeting.

> • Inform your friends, giving as much notice as possible, if you're not going to attend an event. It's better to let them know early, even if they are disappointed, rather than face their anger or upset if you just don't show up.

As individuals, we are connected to people through a number of different social networks. Maintaining contact with them all, sometimes in only 10 days a month, can be a complex matter. People who are particularly close to you form a 'network of significant others'. This includes a spouse or partner, parents, close friends, and other family members. 'Exchange networks' are those people who provide material or symbolic support and include an employer, a childminder, or a GP. 'Interactive networks' are those with whom interactions typically occur. These are the everyday interactions with friends, colleagues, and acquaintances who may also be members of other networks. Crew should take care not to forget who is at the centre of these networks—the self. There is no 'right way' of doing this as every individual has their own requirements for satisfying their personal and social needs.

There will be times when crew experience a conflict arising from dual pressures to simultaneously meet up with differing family members or friends. Imagine that you have been invited to two differing events both at the exact same time and that you have actually managed to get the day off from work. What do you do? It is, of course, almost physically impossible to be in two places at the same time and therefore you may be 'forced' to choose one engagement above the other. This might be accompanied by a fear of 'making' one person feel less valued than the other and concerns about losing friends, upsetting the family, or 'being perceived by others as selfish'. Perhaps a careful consideration of the value attached to each of the relationships involved and the actual events themselves can help you to derive a sensible conclusion from such difficult choices.

Consider these questions when making complex choices

- If choosing between two events, which of them is the most significant to you (e.g. going to a wedding or a birthday party?)
- If choosing between two groups of people, which is more supportive, loyal, or close to you?
- Who is more likely to feel disappointed, upset, or angry with you if you don't attend?
- Can you rearrange a meeting with the group you're not going to get to see? Who will have greater flexibility in their own social calendar to meet up with you on a differing day.

Case study

Phillip had been working as cabin crew for nearly two years when he sought help from a psychologist for stress-related problems. He explained that after he had started his job, he found it difficult to maintain relationships, and was thinking about leaving the profession. He had recently lost contact with his best friend after failing to attend his wedding because of work commitments. Phillip had forgotten to request the day off from work in time and had felt reluctant to tell his friend because he did not want to upset him. Though they used to see each other regularly, this was more difficult now that Phillip was working shifts. When friends got together Philip would rarely be able to join them and this made him feel guilty and anxious. He considered himself as 'an outsider', an inadequate friend, and a less likeable individual. As a result, he would often withdraw from both his friends and colleagues at work because of fear of being rejected once people discovered his 'social flaws'. Although work could be seen as the initial trigger for Philips

> problem, it was his negative perception of his own qualities as a person (inadequate, less likeable) and his avoidant behaviour (withdrawal, failing to answer calls) that served to maintain existing relationship difficulties.

Crews' own change of circumstances can also have an impact on the ability to maintain a new relationship. A growing number of demands compete for the limited time that is available and under such circumstances, crew are required to make complex decisions to decide what to focus on. Of course, there are no absolute rules as to how people should juggle their responsibilities, though prioritisation is an important technique to help to make difficult choices. Prioritising can help with time management but can also lead to longer term solutions. For example, prioritising some friendships over others will eventually lead to a smaller social network, which in the longer run can ease the pressures of keeping in regular contact with many people.

When goal setting goes awry, some relationships inevitably suffer. For example, devoting the majority of spare time to a partner at the expense of other friendships may have a negative outcome if that particular relationship ends. Unlike ground workers, who are usually in close proximity to their social networks, crew are more likely to feel deprived of such support. When an individual leaves home to travel abroad, they are also leaving behind their friends, family, a partner, and other services that support them, such as their GP or other health services. All of these might be relied upon during times of personal difficulty. In the absence of a helpful network of friends and family, enduring a separation or a divorce from one's partner may increase the risks of psychological disturbance. Though spare time should provide ample opportunities to build new social relationships, irregular work patterns make it more difficult for crew to meet new people. Fatigue can influence motivation to go out and meet people.

Conclusion

The irregular patterns of work and the frequent absence from home can make it difficult for crew to develop and maintain social relationships at home. When this is compounded by pressures of managing one's sleep pattern as well as the constant changing crew composition at work, crew are often left with the complex task of dealing with a multitude of simultaneous stressors all at once. This can be emotionally tiring for a majority of people and perhaps more so for those crew who do not possess a solid foundation for social support during times of personal struggles. Close relationships can help people deal better with their everyday problems, and are therefore a vital 'tool' for maintaining a healthy wellbeing. Many people are also engaged in intimate relationships with a husband, a wife, or a partner. Some crew are happily married with children whereas others may struggle to develop a solid foundation for mutual sharing, support, and satisfaction. The next chapter deals with intimate relationships in the context of the aircrew profession. Although each partnership is essentially unique, the aircrew work schedule can sometimes influence, for better or for worse, the overall dynamics of intimate living.

CHAPTER FIVE

Intimate relationships

Being away from home for days or weeks at a time inevitably makes it harder to establish and then maintain romantic relationships. In this section, we discuss the effects of the aircrew lifestyle on personal relationships. Each partnership is different and there are couple-specific features that cannot be generalised across everyone's situation. However, the tensions are eased if a partner can sympathise with the realities of the aircrew profession. This section also outlines some recent research that has looked at the link between aircrew 'marriage' and mental health. It will also highlight supportive psychological resources that are available for crew who are experiencing problems in their relationships.

Selecting a partner

Meeting a prospective partner is not that easy for anyone, regardless of their profession. The difficulty may be greater for aircrew when various factors come together. Work schedules are much more likely to conflict as non-crew members usually work long hours during the week and then have weekends to themselves. Crew, by contrast, are often away for weekends with whole days off during the week.

Consider this imagined scenario, which is one that a crew member might face: Someone you have met at a friend's birthday party suggests going out for dinner the following Friday evening. You would quite like to see this person again, but are scheduled to travel to Singapore in the early hours of Saturday morning. Although you really want to see this person you are worried about having to leave early because of work commitments. What do you do?

- Decline the invitation saying that you are 'too busy', even though this may not send the signals you intend to?
- Explain that you have a long duty day on Saturday morning and try to rearrange the dinner? This may be a better approach as by doing so, you also start the process of educating other people about your work schedule. At the same time, you are showing that you are still interested in taking the relationship further.
- Accept the invitation and try to get plenty of rest during the lead up to your date, possibly sacrificing other tasks or arrangements to keep this one?

People who do not fly are unlikely to fully understand the pressures associated with the profession. They may have misconceptions too, based on stereotypical views that are far removed from the reality of the job. How do you explain the less glamorous side of your profession? How do you communicate that 'crew parties', 'late night drinking' and 'permanent holidays' are not how you would describe your job? It may not always be so easy to explain the negative effects of sleep deprivation and social disruptions to people who have no direct experience of it. 'Hello, I am a pilot who is often tired and lonely because of my work schedule' may not be a great opener for conversations . UK based pilots and cabin crew agreed in interviews that they can overcome this difficulty by gradually educating others about the more difficult aspects of their job. The following points may be worth remembering when communicating your work schedule to non-flyers:

- Try to communicate a balanced view that outlines the positives and negative aspects of your job. All jobs have their good and bad sides and the fact that yours does too may not come as a surprise to anyone.
- Start with the positives as these are the features of your profession that others may be familiar with.
- Be truthful about the negative aspects of your job. Talk about the tiredness, the jetlag, homesickness and the potential difficulties you may encounter when attempting to plan ahead etc.
- Have a positive attitude. If you enjoy your work, don't be too pessimistic about it.

Certain personalities will find it harder to sympathise and empathise with the challenges that aircrew face. An insecure person may find it harder to adjust to your frequent absences than someone who is more confident and secure. Moreover, low levels of independence could cause another person to feel rejected or even abandoned every time you leave home. In a functioning relationship, a partner will gradually learn to deal with the peculiar aspects of the job. Those who struggle to do so may need further reassurance and having to repeatedly comfort someone who is insecure, jealous, or overly dependant is may be an additional pressure for some crew.

- Consider bringing your partner with you on a trip. This will let they see for themselves both the positive and negative aspects of your job. Many airlines offer staff discount for partners, friends, and relatives that will help to keep the costs down. Different airlines have different eligibility criteria for such perks, so consider the financial impact before extending any invitations.

- Keep in regular contact with a partner when you are away. Large time differences can make this more difficult, but other media like text messages or emails are options.
- Prepare your partner for potential complications well in advance.

Tips to help a new partner understand your job:

Some crew meet their partners at work or end up dating other crew members. This may be a different kind of relationship than one that develops between two people who work in the same office. While the latter couple will see each other regularly both at home and at work, crew who enter into a partnership with a colleague will rarely work together on the same flight unless they arrange for it to be this way. In fact, they may struggle to find time together because of their different work schedules and end up facing a different challenge: the *passing ships phenomenon* where weeks or months go by without seeing each other. Requesting corresponding annual leave may be one way to try and spend more time together. This will help to synchronise work patterns so that partners share the same rest periods at home.

Developing a partnership

People bring different characteristics to their relationships, different motives, different personalities, and tendencies to think, feel, and behave in particular ways under particular circumstances. The relationship which result are unsurprisingly also unique and there are no set rules for the way any relationship should progress. Some couples get married while others choose not to, some have children and some do not, and some couples weather significant difficulties with their relationship while others separate or get divorced. Though people actively construct the specifics of their relationship, they do so in broadly similar forms. The details depend on their social and economic situations and are strongly influenced by the current dominant beliefs, culture and ideologies of close relationships. Relationships don't operate in a vacuum and a couple is constantly interacting with their outside environment. The environment includes each person's type of work and the professional demands they experience may disrupt the time available for intimacy, and shared activities.

Many crew may wonder how the lengthy periods of physical absence from home can influence and shape their partnerships. Most relationships are founded on a mutual trust and security. Establishing this foundation in the face of repeated absences from each other is not easy. The initial spark between two people can be short lasting if they don't see each other often enough to explore those feelings and develop a bond. Crew can choose to address this by devoting the majority of their spare time to nurturing the relationship, which in turn could increase the likelihood that it becomes something more long lasting. As time is finite, this approach isn't without its sacrifices and an effort here may mean even less time to see friends, or family or to manage the negative effects of jetlag and fatigue. When faced with these choices, it's not surprising that crew feel pressured to make complex, and often paradoxical, decisions between friends or partners, which can have negative consequences.

The accelerating revolving door syndrome is a term used to describe a strategy commonly used by pilots and cabin crew to speed up the growth of their personal relationships in the wake of serious time limitations. In interviews, crew explained how moving in with a partner shortly after meeting them gave an opportunity to 'test out' the potential of the relationship. This approach might directly reflect the quickened pace of the crew lifestyle overall when compared to other professions.

Rapid progression in a partnership has its practical motives, allowing a couple to assess quite quickly whether together they can cope with the realities of the aircrew lifestyle. The crew member may face difficult decisions between seeing friends or being with a partner. Similarly, the non-crew partner may change existing plans to fit their partner's erratic ones. Having a close relationship early on with a partner may make it easier to make choices. For example, if the relationship is considered to be 'inappropriate' at an early stage, crew might be less inclined to jeopardise friendships. Alternatively, one might be more willing to sacrifice social events if the partnership is proving to be something more worthwhile. Having an early understanding of the degree of compatibility between yourself and a partner might prevent *double losses*. Uk crew spoke of many situations whereby they had devoted a majority of their time to a partner and found themselves with very few friends left when the relationship broke down. In the absence of a supportive network of friends and family, any separation may be more difficult to handle and such situations could lead to a greater risk of grief or depression for even the most resilient crew member.

The *accelerating revolving door syndrome* has its negative consequences too. Crew who suggest rapid development in a relationship might be thought of as needy or dependant by their partners. Making serious commitments during the beginning phase of a relationship isn't necessarily an appealing style to all people. Given that a majority of other professionals might not be familiar with the hasty pace of the crew lifestyle, some people might also feel overwhelmed or intimidated by the prospect of fast developments and quick commitments.

Case study

Thomas and Sarah had been going out for 6 months when Sarah suggested they should move in together. Thomas said he was not 'ready' to make this kind of commitment. He would like to 'get to know' Sarah a bit better before they developed their relationship. Sarah, a long-haul cabin crew member, found it difficult to understand why Thomas would not commit to her. She felt she had dedicated all her time in-between trips to being with Thomas and was wondering what 'more he could possible want from her'. Thomas, on the other hand, said that he was 'happy with the way things were going' and suggested that Sarah was becoming 'hasty' and 'impatient'. Sarah then started to feel personally rejected and accused Thomas of not wanting to be with her. In her past relationships, Sarah had always lived with her partners shortly after meeting them. She thought that this would allow more time for being with her boyfriends in-between her travels. Thomas, on the other hand, had never lived with any of his previous girlfriends. He found the prospect of sharing a home with someone else overwhelming, especially since he had only been going out with Sarah for six months. Their unique relationship history had led Thomas and Sarah to develop a differing belief about the pace of commitments and developments within a companionship. The discrepancy between slow versus fast couple evolvements led each partner to feel 'threatened' by the other person's suggestion.

Maintaining a partnership

There can be some complex learning required for both people in a partnership. It is important for both people to be empathetic to the difficulties the others are experiencing. In an attempt to understand why it might be hard for their partner to accept frequent absences for example, crew could remind themselves about what they had to learn during the initial stages of their job.

The following questions may help to reflect on your own experience.

- What did you feel when you were away from home? Did you miss your friends and family?
- How did you deal with the difficulties to do with planning ahead? Did you become more organised or did you schedule social events around your work schedule?
- How did you maintain contact with relatives and friends?
- Was there a point when you learned how to make personal life fit work? If so, are there any specific techniques that may be worth sharing with your partner?

Absence may make the *heart grow fonder* for some people, but physical separations for extended periods can increase a sense of emotional distance or strangeness within a partnership. This can be more obvious immediately after returning home from long periods abroad. A partner may need to get used to having you home again, or you are taking time to adjust to being out of work mode. Crew might struggle with having to make repeated switches between independent functioning and being more co-dependent when they are at home with their partner. Achieving the right balance can be difficult.

Case study

Paul and William sought help for relationship difficulties including heated arguments over various things ranging from domestic responsibilities to financial commitments. They explained that they rarely agreed on anything anymore. William said he was 'fed up' by Paul's accusations of him having an affair every time he returned from duty travels abroad. Paul, in turn, accused William of acting 'cold and distant' which he interpreted as evidence of infidelity. When asked about their disagreements, they revealed that the arguments often took place immediately after William's return from a period of absence from home. While William attributed this to Paul's jealous behaviour, Paul felt that William's mood was like a 'ticking' time bomb waiting to explode. He believed that William was not glad to see him again, and that he would rather be with his crew colleagues than at home with his partner. William agreed that he was sometimes irritable after work but explained that this was due to lack of sleep rather than his feelings towards Paul. Neither partner was able to deal appropriately with the absences from one and another, and this perpetuated their current relationship difficulties.

The repeated process of leaving home, often for several days at a time, can generate an emerging sense of a *stop and start* cycle in relationships. Crew might relate to the sentiment of having to 'get to know' their partners again each time they see them. such insecurities may be compounded by circumstances where it might not be possible to devote enough time to maintain the relationship. Some people may tend towards over-compensations for their partner's feeling of rejection. This includes crew buying excessive gifts to appease their own sense of guilt during time away from their partner.

The crew themselves may also find it hard to leave someone they care about behind. They may experience high levels of frustration and homesickness, which can make it harder to leave for a trip, especially when there are existing difficulties within their relationships. Interestingly, crew felt that emotionally turbulent times were a natural result of intimate relationships including *differences in outlook and beliefs* rather than as a direct consequence of the job itself. It may be harder for crew to deal with problems in their relationships than it is for people with other jobs because of their physical absences. Some crew may still feel frustrated because they can't immediately *patch things up with their partners*. This can lead to worry and anxiety whilst away on a trip, particularly if there are limited opportunities to stay in contact with family and friends at home.

Fatigue may also complicate crews' ability to cope with domestic stress upon return home, and worrying about unresolved issues can in turn exacerbate tiredness. Sleep deprivation can magnify any alleged problems at home and make it difficult to think rationally. Arguments upon return from a trip are not uncommon. It is important to try and get adequate rest before starting conversations about highly emotional topics with a partner.

Case study

Sue had not slept properly for the entire duration of her trip. She had been worried about a recent argument with her partner and was keen to 'try and patch things up' as soon as she returned.

When she got home, her partner Simon was having breakfast in the lounge. Sue immediately began discussing their relationship but Simon refused to enter into a debate as he knew she would be tired from working through the night. He suggested that Sue went to bed for a couple of hours and that they could discuss relationship issues when she felt less tired and emotional. Sue immediately burst into tears telling Simon that she 'just wanted to sort things out'. Simon explained to Sue that he too wanted to talk through the incident but he felt that the discussion would be more constructive when Sue was rested and alert. When Sue had caught up on some sleep, she realised that the argument was less significant than it had felt during the layover period abroad.

Relationships and coping

Why are relationships important? Secure relationships, particularly with a companion who is supportive, can improve wellbeing and reduce stress levels. Research into this issue has shown that people who have support from their partner or close friends are more likely to resist the damaging effects of stressful life events such as bereavement, an accident, a physical illness, or other personal crises.

The effects that disruptions in personal relationships can have on the mental health of aircrew are not properly understood and fully appreciated. Some studies have shown that relationship support is important for aircrew performance, but fewer have focussed specifically on the link between relationships and crews' emotional wellbeing. Crew who have a supportive partner at home may find it easier to manage sleep deprivation because their partner is more sympathetic towards their need for rest. Conversely, crew who are experiencing relationship problems may find that their work is affected, particularly if they spend their time worrying about personal issues during long duty hours abroad.

The mental health of aircrew pilots have been found to be closely associated with the degree of autonomy or control they feel they have at work. It may also be affected by their levels of fatigue, and the degree of social support around them. Those crew that lack sufficient support from a significant life partner or spouse may not cope as well with life events as those who have this support. Family, friends, and a partner are an indispensable social support system. Surveys of shift-working nurses and their partners, showed that their partner's understanding of their needs (e.g., sleep, fatigue) and their own sense of personal disruption was critical to the shift worker's ability to establish a work-life balance.

Relationship difficulties, whether they are due to stress, physical separation or other reasons for conflict, are amenable to counselling. Mental health professionals can play an important role in helping aircrew to deal with the wider impacts of work requirements on their personal relationships. When helping couples, they are likely to consider the unique stressors that each partner are facing and try to help them restore supportive interactions. There are different types of support available to suit different people's requirements and wishes; couple therapy can be offered for both the crew member and their partner together, individual therapy can focus on enhancing communication, satisfaction, and social support within the relationship, or more practical advice can be given such as providing details on access to various forms of psychological interventions in the NHS, private setting, or other specific helping organisations. These interventions may help to reduce emotional stress associated with problems in relationships, and can buffer against ill health in the workplace.

Conclusion

This chapter has drawn on the experience of aircrew and pilots themselves to put some context around the pressures of romantic relationships. Though stable relationships can help reduce the negative effects of work stress, aircrew might find it difficult to get to that place with their partner because of the unique pressures of their job. The next chapter presents an overall view of the aircrew lifestyle. Whereas many of the other chapters have sought to offer an in-depth discussion of a single aspect of an aircrew member's life, the forthcoming section is pre-dominantly about the holistic nature of work-life balances. It is hoped that the reader will benefit from the various practical guidelines pertaining to the art of 'making personal life fit work'.

CHAPTER SIX

Achieving a work-life balance

Having a healthy balance between work and life outside of work is important for physical and mental wellbeing. It is not easy to achieve this balance when a job is demanding. In this chapter there will be a brief introduction to work stress before considering the recent trends in the aviation industry that have intensified aircrew workloads and working hours. The chapter presents strategies to help individuals achieve a work-life balance and concludes with a 'mini-theory' on how to 'make personal life fit work' based on accounts given by cabin crew and flight crew across major UK and European airlines. A large proportion of the available literature tends to focus on factors that cause work stress, work-life conflict, and psychological imbalance. While this is helpful, there is a need for more focus on positive actions to achieve balance within a given lifestyle. A more pragmatic approach may help those who are trying to combine work and family demands, and allow them to learn techniques to cope with threats to their physical and mental health. Practical tips on how to manage conflicting life stressors are given.

Work stress and commercial aviation

Stress is the way people feel when they are under too much pressure. It is the psychological and physical state that result when the resources of the individual are insufficient to cope with the demands and pressure of the situation. Work stress has become a major concern in recent years because of the potential impact on employee wellbeing and performance. Studies have shown that a moderate amount of pressure can be positive; making people feel more alert, helping to maintain motivation and improving their performance. However, too much pressure, or prolonged pressure, can lead to stress. Although stress has been classified in different ways over the years, the generally accepted terminology today is one that includes an interaction between a situation or context and an individual.

The negative effects of stress include physical ones—raised blood pressure, heart disease, headaches, nausea and indigestion. Emotional problems may also arise, including anxiety, depression, anger, and fear. Stress may also alter people's behaviour leading them to become withdrawn, indecisive or inflexible. Tearfulness, and irritability can also occur and libido may be affected.

Airline workers are not alone in facing challenges at work. However, their environment means that their challenges are quite unique. Competition in commercial aviation is high because of the success of new, low-cost airlines such as Southwest airlines, Easy Jet and Ryanair. Resultant increases in workloads and the pressures of absences from home and jetlag and fatigue, can have implications for aircraft and passenger safety.

Not all stressors are under an individual's direct control. Aircrew must have support at both an individual and an organisational level to keep this in check. Individual approaches could include further training in assertiveness skills, time management and problem solving so employees can manage their daily strains better. Organisations should ensure that their structures (staffing levels, work schedules) are fair and within legal parameters and could provide staff with more control over their work patterns and offer other forms of support as required (e.g. counselling). Approaches to stress management that concentrate on changing the individual without changing the sources of stress may not be effective. Someone who, for example, is experiencing stress related symptoms as a result of limited control over their work schedule will only be helped in the short term by sickness leave. Stress may return once the individual goes back to work again.

Work-life conflict

When work related pressures compete with activities outside of work or vice versa, there is a work-life conflict. This process of negative interactions between work and home is thought to happen in three ways. Firstly, demands may make it physically impossible to be in two places at the same time, e.g. when periods abroad prevent participation in family activities. Alternatively, strain may spill over from one domain to another, e.g. when work related anxiety makes it harder to relax at home. Thirdly, there may be incompatibility between behaviours expected at work compared with what is expected at home. Some crew, for example, may find it hard to stop acting independently up on their return to family or a partner.

Having conflict between these two very important domains can have an effect on physical and mental wellbeing. For organisations, work-life conflict is associated with absenteeism, high staff turnover, reduced performance and lower organisational commitment. It is certainly not uncommon in the commercial aviation industry. For individuals, the pressures can build up and seem unbearable.

Ask yourself

- What types of life situations are most likely to affect you? An argument with a friend or partner? Inability to achieve personal goals? Physical health issues? The death of a close relative? Being single?

- How do you react? Sad, angry, frustrated, anxious or calm and collected?
- Are these reactions intensified during events of fatigue? For example, when you return from a flight do you sometimes feel sadder than you usually would if you were dealing with an upsetting situation whilst awake and alert?
- What actions to you take to improve the situation or make yourself feel better about the situation? Talk to someone, or engage in other activities to distract you from thinking too much about the situation, or avoid the issue all in all hoping that 'everything will be ok again'.
- Does the experience of fatigue make it more difficult (or not) to deal with pressing situations?

The degree of psychological disturbance that results from trying to reconcile these seemingly incompatible pressures depends upon some quite complex decision making processes. When making choices, individuals weigh up the consequences of making one particular decision over another. The way these decisions are reached is also very specific to the individual. Although this seems logical, considering everyone's unique experiences, it's not clear whether this is because people are motivated differently in the first place, have different roles in their company (which may affect their degree of work control), or have a stronger social support network around them.

Identifying your stressors

- Try to identify the factors that are causing you stress. Consider making a list or a map of these factors. Links between some stressors may become apparent.
- Rate your stress factors, using a simple scale (high to low stress). This may help you to make some choices more

easily. For example, if cleaning the house is less important (low stress) than meeting a friend for lunch (high stress) you could leave domestic duties for another day.
- Prioritise the tasks on your list. This could help you to make choices between them if time is limited.
- Consider the longer-term consequences of your decisions.

Aircrew must be creative to achieve their work-life balance and learning how to do this properly takes time. Managing time appropriately is crucial.

Theories about coping

Crew must use a range of creative techniques to achieve their work-life balance. It is interesting to consider this in the context of what professionals believe to be universal coping strategies that most people use. Some say that an individual who is faced with threats of physical or psychological illnesses will be motivated to maintain some kind of equilibrium. The skills used to deal with the situation will determine the outcome, that of wellbeing or deterioration. This and other theories may not be sufficient to explain the experience of aircrew, particularly the processes they initiate to deal with threats of psychological disturbance. For aircrew, there are significant inter-relationships between various stressors and being able to cope in such complex situations requires particular decision-making skills. The following diagrams represent graphically the situation for crew who are faced with a relatively rigid work schedule and must adapt their social lives (e.g. be very flexible) around this. The work-life balance becomes more of an attempt to make life fit in with work.

Before crew proceed to cope, they appear to learn, perhaps through experience, that their work schedules are inflexible. In the figures below, this is represented by the straight line.

Once they learn this, they begin to recognise the advantages of sculpturing their own self around their work. This is illustrated in figure 2 below. Achieving this high level of individual fluidity, as illustrated by the progressive relationship in figure 3, plays a major role in the establishment of a work-life balance.

There are knock on effects of changes in one's personal life. Someone who is married, for example, may choose to rest during their layover period to ensure they have more time for their partner while at home. The process of making personal life fit work is a dynamic rather than a static phenomenon. The individual is essentially required to deal with many transitional stages that comprise their 'private life' whilst

Figure 1. The static nature of the Crew work schedule.

Figure 2. The dynamic and fluid nature of adjustments to work.

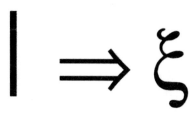

Figure 3. The progression from static to dynamic coping.

simultaneously making sure that each change fits in with the requirements of their work.

Case study

Paul, a commercial airline pilot, sought help from a counsellor for stress-related problems. He had recently transferred to short-haul operations having spent over 12 years on the long-haul fleet. He lived with his wife, Jenny, and two children in a small village about 200 miles from work. Paul explained that the transfer was a mandatory part of his promotion (Captain command), and that he was now required to drive to work at least 5 times a week. Jenny was reluctant to move closer to the airport because she did not wish to move away from friends, family, and her work. Paul, on the other hand, found it difficult to cope with the long drive to work and felt Jenny was being unreasonable. He would often decline social engagements with friends and family due to early wake ups and late finishes at work. It appeared that Paul's initial problem with adjusting to recent changes in his work life had triggered off high levels of stress which in turn disrupted familial and social relationships at home. Once he became secure in his new job role and accustomed to the long drives, Paul continued to make very little effort with his wife and friends. As a result, his stress level remained high until he was able to deal with the strains of fragile relations in his home life.

If the stress factors are grouped, difficulties in one ultimately influence each of the remaining groups. The diagram below illustrates the relationship between these competing stress factors. As can be seen, developing a new relationship may require crew to spend time with the other person, which in turn may require spending less time with friends at home and using time

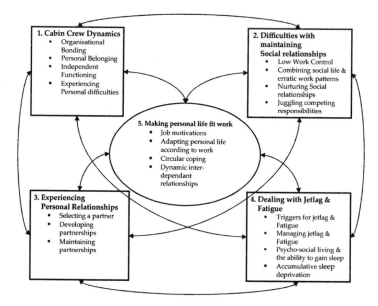

Figure 4. Aircrew competing pressures.

abroad to rest instead of socialising. Failure to pay attention to all of the facets can increase risk of stress, burn out, and psychological disturbance. In interviews, crew suggest that this delicate balancing act means that their adjustments may be greater than those needed by the majority of other professions.

As there is less room for flexibility with work schedules, crew usually address their work-life balance by actively managing those aspects of their personal lives that are more independent of work. Crew exercise some selection over which tasks they can juggle, though not much is known about how this is done. In interviews, crew explained how they develop ways to adapt to adverse circumstances after years of experience. It is possible that the unbending work schedules mean that crew must compensate by doing even more on their own to manage their work stress. Crew should not underestimate their strategies and the skills they draw on to ensure a work-life balance, happiness, and wellbeing.

Ask yourself:

- What strategies do I use to remain in regular contact with friends and family?
- How do I ensure adequate time for my partner and children?
- What do I do when I can't get a specific day off from work?
- How do I deal with disruptions to my work schedule because of operational delays?
- Do I dedicate enough time for myself or am I forever running around chasing personal obligations at home?
- What techniques do I use to manage disrupted sleep?
- How do I deal with personal difficulties when going to work?
- Which activities help me to stay fit and healthy during my travels?

Personality traits such as social cooperation, friendliness, and openness are pivotal to crews' experience of team dynamics. Social competence and good team work are important during safety procedures and emergency situations, or when handling difficult passengers. Social flexibility and friendliness are important to bond rapidly with new colleagues and to manage one's position in such fluid groups. Close work relationships, though they might not last long, can be a supportive substitute for the absence of a social network. Of course, not all crew have exceptional inter-personal qualities, but those that don't may find it harder to fit into and function with a group of unknown colleagues on board an aircraft.

Case study

Sarah got on well with her colleagues on the outbound flight to Singapore and was thought of as a friendly and sociable. During the layover period she socialised with the rest of the crew, went to the cinema, and did some shopping. During the busy shuttle flight to Sydney, the crew had to deal with two medical emergencies. Although Sarah was not dealing with the medical incidents herself, she felt increasingly stressed throughout the flight. She snapped at her colleagues, argued with passengers, and appeared aggressive towards her supervisor. The crew around her was feeling increasingly tired of her behaviour and the group dynamics was gradually becoming more fragile and hostile by the minute. When arriving at the hotel in Sydney, a majority of the crew was eager to escape and quickly checked-in to their respective rooms. Once Sarah arrived in her hotel room, she realised that her behaviour onboard the aircraft had been inappropriate. She felt increasingly ashamed and embarrassed towards her colleagues. When she awoke in the morning she called several crew members to arrange meeting for breakfast. Each colleague declined her invitation leaving Sarah feeling rejected, disliked and increasingly homesick.

Conclusion

Managing the aircrew lifestyle can be difficult. The irregular patterns of work can disrupt crews' ability to plan ahead and organise their personal lives. Moreover, the frequent absence from home can often restrict crews' opportunities for being with partners, friends, and family. This can lead to work-life conflict whereby crew may essentially feel 'torn' between work requirements and home demands. The chapter presents recommendations to help 'make personal life fit work'. The first thing is to identify the root of the problem before confronting it head on. Time management, prioritisations, creative thinking, constructive decision making and organisational skills are essential techniques that can prevent work-life conflict. In the next chapter, Martin Casey, a commercial airline pilot and an active sport enthusiast, discusses physical health, presenting a realistic picture of the threats to health that exist at 35.000 feet. He goes on to discuss the link between exercise and wellbeing. The reader will benefit from a range of practical guidelines on how they can improve their fitness level, health, and motivation while at home and during layover periods abroad.

CHAPTER SEVEN

Physical health

Martin Casey

Most people these days have been on a long haul flight. Recent expansions in the aviation industry have meant an increase in the number of flights and destinations offered to the public. This has resulted in greater opportunities for both business travel and leisure, though few people are airborne as much as professional aircrew. There are greater pressures on crew to operate more flights and work longer hours than ever before. This means that most major airlines are likely to roster employees toward the upper legal limits of flying. To date, the maximum number of flying hours permitted for UK aircrew is 900 hours in any rolling twelve month period as set by the Civil Aviation Authority. Overseas airlines may be subject to different maximum permitted flying hours because they are governed by different aviation authorities (JAA or FAA). The annual flying time limit translates as follows into actual time in the air:

900 hours = 37.5 days per year in the air

So if a crew member works for 10 years then they would spend:

10 x 37.5 = 375 days > 1 year in the air

Spending one year in ten of one's life airborne is far from an insignificant amount of time. Many questions immediately arise:

- Is the workplace environment safe and healthy?
- What health factors are crew exposed to?
- Is there anything crew can do to lessen any risks?

This chapter will discuss some of the challenging factors which affect the working crew member. In reality they just skim the surface of a vast subject area, but the aim here is to cover the common ones and to dispel some of the many myths which people may have heard.

The workplace environment

Undoubtedly, the workplace of a professional crew member is different to that of an office employee. Regular air travel over long distances can have an effect on both health and well being. The following environmental factors may affect aircrew:

- Changes in cabin air pressure
- Low cabin humidity levels
- Ozone exposure
- Cosmic radiation exposure
- Immobility and associated circulatory problems (DVT)

Crew members must pass stringent medical checks before they are accepted for their job on the aircraft and are assumed therefore to be able to operate within this environment without fear (see chapter eight). People with pre-existing health problems are most likely to be affected, and they usually require consultation with a medical professional before flying. Each crew member receives medical training before work begins and will therefore be aware of the health factors associated with flying.

Crew members often discuss the environmental factors that affect their health. Such conversations are common:

'So-did you hear about that crew member who collapsed in the aisle because of the low cabin air pressure?'

'Someone told me that crew may be at higher risk of developing colds and nasal problems because of the cabin humidity levels'

Do any of these rumours ring bells? You may have had conversations about them yourself or heard other people talking about them. How does flying really affect your physical health and wellbeing? In the following section, there are brief descriptions of the environmental factors that crew are exposed to and a discussion about the potential effects that each can have.

Cabin air pressure

Modern aircraft usually fly at heights between 30,000 and 40,000 feet. At these altitudes the air contains significantly less oxygen than at the altitudes most people spend their lives in.

Other people may be exposed to the challenges of high altitude. When a mountain climber, for example, attempts to climb Everest (29,028 ft) they need to first acclimatise slowly to the extreme altitude and also use portable oxygen tanks when nearing the summit to avoid 'altitude sickness' and the serious effects associated with lack of oxygen. Hypoxia is the medical term that refers to a lack of oxygen in the tissues. The onset of hypoxia at extreme altitudes is very rapid and can have serious consequences.

To avoid such problems all large modern passenger aircraft have pressurized cabins. Un-pressurized small commercial aircraft cannot fly at high altitudes. Air is taken from the vast amount passing through the engines, filtered, temperature regulated and pumped into the cabin of the aircraft to create an environment in the cabin that is similar to one at lower altitudes. The cabin pressure is equivalent to an outside air pressure at 5000–8000 ft dependent upon the specific aircraft and its cruising level.

As they spend so much time in this environment, crew in effect spend much of their working life 'at altitude' where there is less oxygen available in the air to be taken into the blood. Importantly, these oxygen levels are considered sufficient and well tolerated by healthy crew and passengers and the advantages of having a healthy respiratory system and blood flow are clear.

As the aircraft climbs to its cruising altitude the pressure in the aircraft cabin reduces from sea level pressure to that equivalent to 8000 ft. This reduction in air pressure causes the gases in the body to expand. This gas expansion is equalised in the body by air passing out through the sinuses and the middle ear. In descent, the opposite occurs, with the increase in aircraft cabin pressure causing the gases in the body to contract. Again air usually flows back in through the same path ways. Discomfort, pain or injury may occur if crew have ear, nose or throat illnesses that prevent this equalisation from happening.

Long haul crew members are exposed to high altitudes both on the aircraft and at some of the destinations they travel to. For example, Mexico City sits at an altitude of 7,200 ft. Crew who are not used to such altitudes may experience dizziness and faintness when exercising and some gyms carry warnings to this effect.

Cabin humidity

Humidity is the amount of water in the air and when describing environments, the usual index of relative humidity is quoted. Relative humidity is a useful index of dryness or dampness of an environment. In a normal household, the relative humidity is usually in excess of 30%. In an aircraft, humidity is considerably lower, usually less than 20%. Crew are regularly exposed to this level of humidity and often experience dry skin and discomfort to the eyes, mouth and nose because of this. The following can help to reduce these discomforts:

- Regular use of a skin moisturizer
- Wearing spectacles rather than contact lenses
- Use of a saline nasal spray
- Avoiding too many caffeinated drinks
- Keeping well hydrated by drinking water

Exposure to ozone

Ozone is a gas which contains 3 atoms of oxygen per molecule (O_3) rather than the 2 atoms which occurs in free oxygen (O_2). At about 6–30 miles above the earth is an atmospheric layer that contains a high concentration of ozone—the ozone layer. This layer has a crucial function, to absorb ultra violet radiation (UV) from the sun, protecting the earth and its inhabitants from exposure to too much of these potentially harmful rays.

The higher concentrations found at altitude can be harmful to humans. The levels found in older aircraft caused lung irritation, and discomfort of the eyes and nasal tissues. Modern passenger aircraft, however, are designed in such a way that the risks of exposure to ozone are greatly reduced. Catalytic converters and air filters clean the air which enters the cabin environment, and break down the ozone, pumping out the by-products and any associated odours.

Cosmic radiation

Cosmic rays are high speed particles that travel towards the earth from their point of origin, the sun and the solar system. Infrequent air travel doesn't significantly increase exposure to these cosmic rays. However, crew who spend significant amounts of time at the high altitudes at which modern aircraft fly are exposed to higher levels of cosmic radiation. The effects of this degree exposure are unclear and more research is being done on this. Some studies suggest a link between high levels of cosmic radiation and increased risks of cancer, cataracts, damage to DNA and neurological disorders.

Immobility and circulation

Passengers know that immobility during long flights can increase the risk of circulation problems and in serious cases, thrombosis. There is an increasing commercial pressure on airlines and many attempt to maximise the number of passengers they carry. This efficiency drive means cabin crew members have many tasks to perform and are on their feet and moving around for the majority of the flight. The first time many get to sit down is at the start of their allocated in-flight rest. This constant movement keeps the blood flowing and has positive effects.

For security reasons, the cockpit is a highly protected environment. Pilots may feel reluctant to leave the flight deck and feel the effects of spending time in such a restricted space. For pilots, who spend many hours sitting in the same position, there can be long periods of immobility.

Immobility can result in swelling, discomfort or stiffness, particularly in the legs where blood can pool. For this reason, pilots should take regular breaks from sitting at the controls of the aircraft, even if only for five minutes to stretch their limbs and change position. This keeps the blood flowing around the body. Most aircraft have an area of some size behind the cockpit seats where this is possible.

Staying healthy

Most crew lead healthy and normal lives, and cope well with the unique challenges of their environment. The usual advice to eat a well balanced diet, supplement with vitamins if necessary and take regular exercise applies to crew, though irregular timing may make it a little more difficult to eat and exercise regularly. Sports clubs and gyms require some regular commitment or fees, so are unsympathetic to erratic schedules. Crew usually have plenty of spare time during their layover to improve their fitness level.

Case study

A crew member has just operated a ten hour flight from London to Hong Kong and has just arrived at his hotel. He is standing in the hotel lobby with colleagues who are discussing what to do that evening. He is feeling energetic, having slept during the in-flight rest, and declares that he will head to the gym for a work out before heading to the bar.

"*You can't do that, it's really bad for you to go to the gym after a flight!*" suggests one of the crew.

"*That'll increase the chances of DVT!*" says another.

"*You shouldn't train until you're over the jet lag, and we're always jet lagged so we should never train!*" says another.

Crew faced with such statements may wonder whether there is any truth in them. Sport and exercise has a wealth of benefits but can seem quite daunting to some. The next section will discuss the benefits of regular exercise, focussing on the advantages of particular exercise types. We will also discuss the positive effects that exercise has on mental wellbeing and how to overcome the negative effects that sleep deprivation have on exercise routines.

Let's get physical

Exercise is associated with many benefits and one way to counter some of the potential health risks associated with flying is through regular exercise. Different people have different exercise thresholds and exercise and physical activity can take many different forms. The airline workforce too is diverse and varied, with ages ranging from 18 to 65 years. Some might consider exercise as carrying a suitcase up two flights of stairs. For others who are used to heavier exercise, a game of rugby meets that definition.

Thirty minutes of moderate activity on most days of the week should be enough to keep healthy. Increasing amounts or intensity of exercise increase the benefits. A brisk fifteen minute walk to a favourite local spot on a lay over destination is exercise. The thirty minute requirement doesn't need to be done all at once, and needn't be performed in the latest sports wear or in a high tech gym.

The Health benefits of regular exercise

Lower risk of heart disease: Regular exercise increases the strength of the heart muscle, increasing its working capacity and improving blood flow. Exercise also reduces the level of bad cholesterol in the blood.

Lower blood pressure: This is partly due to the increased heart muscle strength and capacity associated with exercise, but is also aided by the reduction in body fat and hence blood pressure.

Control of weight: Exercise burns calories and builds or maintains muscle mass, both of which help to control weight. For best results, regular exercise should be combined with a balanced diet. Obesity is associated with many health risks.

Prevention of diabetes (type 2): Reducing the amount of body fat reduces the risk of type 2 diabetes and helps to control the disease for sufferers.

Prevention of osteoporosis: Weight bearing exercises improve bone by increasing bone density. This in turn reduces the risk of osteoporosis.

Lower risk of arthritis: Through a combination of strength and flexibility training the body remains healthy for longer.

Longer and better quality of life: Physical activity keeps a person fit, flexible and mobile, lowers the risk of cardiovascular disease and boosts self confidence enabling a full and more enjoyable life.

There are three main types of exercise:

- Aerobic or cardiovascular
- Resistance or strength
- Flexibility

Each have their own benefits and many sports and activities combine the different types and hence the benefits.

Different types of exercise

Aerobic and cardiovascular exercise

Any exercise which increases the heart rate is aerobic and good for the cardiovascular system, i.e. your heart and blood vessels. Examples include walking, cycling, swimming, running or aerobics. Different factors affect the degree to which the heart rate increases, including age, level of fitness, level of energy. There are different training zones for different reasons, e.g. to burn fat, to increase muscle stamina etc, and individuals have target heart rates that depend upon their reason for doing the exercise and their age.

Modern training equipment in gyms usually display tables suggesting a target heart rate at which to exercise. Though this target is quite person specific, a good rule of thumb is a maximum of 220 beats per minute minus the person's age:

For example: a 44yr old has a suggested maximum heart rate of

$$220 - 44 = 176 \text{ bpm max}$$

These are only guides and each person has individual requirements. The best course of action is to consult a fitness trainer before embarking on any new fitness regimes.

Benefits of different types of exercise

Importantly, some high blood pressure medications lower the maximum heart rate and the recommended target zone. People

---

LIGHT 60–70% of max HR—duration 30–90 mins –

While exercise, breathing should be comfortable and easy, with some associated light sweating. Post-exercise benefits include improvement of basic endurance and recovery ability.

MODERATE 70–80% of max HR—duration 20–60 mins –

While exercising, one should have a steady breathing rate and be able to talk while maintaining the level. Associated sweating is moderate. Moderate exercise is good for the heart and circulation.

HARD 80–90% of max HR—duration 5–20 mins –

While exercise, breathing will be heavy and muscles will feel weighty and tired. This exercise increases the maximum performance thresholds but also should be done with great care as the risk of injury is increased.

---

taking such medication should contact their doctors about the recommended exercise levels.

Though not essential, a simple watch-like heart rate monitor can help you to manage your training intensity. Physical signs, such as changes in breathing rate, muscles and limbs feeling weighty or increased sweating are good indicators that the body is tiring or that exercise intensity is increasing. If you are sweating but can still talk while exercising, you are exercise at about a moderate level of intensity.

Strength training

Strength training is resistance or weight training, using methods to build muscle strength. The 'resistance' could be in the form of weights, a resistance band, or simply ones own body weight, e.g. when doing push ups. Before strength based training it is important to 'warm up' cold muscles to avoid straining them. People using weight equipment in gyms should remember that they are specialised machines that can lead to injury if used incorrectly or inappropriately. Ask advice from onsite staff if you aren't sure how to use the equipment. Fitness instructors can suggest a routine of strength based exercise to suit individual needs. Yoga or circuit classes rely on the body's own weight as the resistance with which to build or maintain muscle strength. Example exercises include squat thrusts, lunges or push ups which tone and condition different body parts.

Regular strength training increases muscle mass and decreases fatty tissues. Muscle is metabolically active, which means it needs calories to function. As we age, we lose muscle which may be replaced by body fat. Fat needs fewer calories to be sustained, so the body needs less calories as it ages. Weight gain results if calorie intake doesn't reduce with this reduction in requirements. Regular strength based exercise can minimise the loss of lean muscle tissue resulting in a healthier, balanced and toned physique and helping to combat the effects of the ageing process.

Flexibility training

Flexibility training stretches the long muscles, increasing the range of motion of the body. Yoga or pilates are examples.

To reduce the risk of injury, it is important to warm up and stretch both before and after workouts or classes.

Effect of exercise on mental wellbeing

Exercise has positive effects on mental wellbeing and putting an effort into a well balanced and planned training structure is associated with a 'feel good factor'. Exercise reduces stress levels, enhances mood, and promote a general sense of well being.

Participation in a sport usually includes learning a skill or a set of skills. The increase in competence and confidence associated with practice can enhance self belief and energy off the sports field too.

Let's take an example of a crew member who is a regular treadmill runner focusing for the last year on reducing their 5 km run time to less than 22 mins. On the day that they achieve that goal, they are bound to feel a great achievement and accomplishment. It may be easier to tackle a difficult work-related challenge later that day because the level of self-belief is high, there is a positive mood and a good attitude.

Not everyone likes exercise, and some crew might find similar benefits attached to achieving very different types of goals, for example completing a distance learning course.

Most sporting activities provide an opportunity for social networking, such as a squash ladder, a swimming club or a team sport. The interactions with like minded individuals that these set ups enable an important supportive network. A major challenge faced by crew is being able to commit to regular sports. Periods of time away from home can be used to a crew member's advantage, e.g. to negotiate discounts at the local gym, or taking advantage of cheaper off-peak memberships. The climate at various destinations could be more suitable for outside activities than during certain seasons at home. By planning and thinking ahead, crew can certainly work an efficient training regime into their work schedules.

Sleep deprivation, disruption and performance

The endurance athlete Paula Radcliffe regularly sleeps for as much as 14 hours per day. The 'Iron Lady', Dame Margaret Thatcher, on the other hand was renowned for requiring just 4 hours each night. Clearly the amount of sleep required is variable and depends upon the individual and what type of activities they are involved in. On average, the 'normal' amount of sleep required ranges from about 5 to 10 hours and those who need less to function won't be as susceptible to problems associated with sleep deprivation. Individuals must 'listen to, and know their own body', and be aware of their own requirements. Consider the follow:

---

10 hrs sleep required – 7 hrs sleep achieved = 3 hrs sleep deficit

7 hrs sleep achieved – 5 hrs sleep required = 2 hrs sleep credit

---

When should I train?

The timing of exercise is important and performance will be affected by whether the body thinks it is day or night. To give oneself the maximum chance of achieving exercise goals, it is best to train during the body's wake cycle.

During the body's sleep cycle, especially during the early morning hours, the core temperature is lowest and exercise will be affected.

With a low core temperature, the individual is likely to feel sluggish, tired and probably won't be functioning at a high level.

Acclimatisation

A suitable training time can help crew to acclimatise to a new time zone. For example, some find that after a large easterly

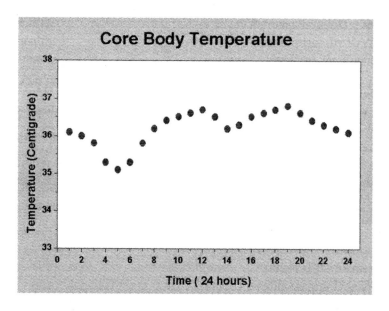

time shift, exercising before midday local time on the first days of arrival discourages acclimatisation. After travel in a westerly direction exercising late in the evening can have an equally negative effect.

Case study

A crew member has had a restless nights sleep on a friend's sofa bed the night before he reported for his duty, a flight from London to Narita. He then wasn't able to sleep on his crew rest as he found the temperature in the bunks uncomfortable. He hasn't slept properly now for two whole days. He has arranged to play squash with evenly matched colleague at 9am in the hotel gym. How do you think he will fair?

The crew member may find that his reaction times are not quite what they usually are. He may not see the ball as quickly as he usually does, and at times he may be indecisive about what shots to play. Chances are he will lose the game.

Why?

1. Having travelled East across many time zones, it would have been better to play a game in the late afternoon. Early in the morning, before having a chance to acclimatise, his body still thinks it is the middle of the night. Back at home, this would be a time when his core body temperature is lowest and his performance is most likely to be affected.

2. There is a significant tendency towards slower visual reaction times with each successive day without sleep. As a sleep deprived individual, a catch up sleep would have helped his game.

3. Studies have shown a close relationship between work rates and the body's core temperature. It would have been better to postpone the game to later in the day when his body was in its wake cycle and hence able to work better.

4. Loss of sleep negatively affects mood. The game would be more enjoyable and successful if he was in a positive frame of mind.

Case study

A London based crew member arrives in Los Angeles late in the afternoon. After a turbulent night of sleep in the hotel she finally decides to get up. The time in Los Angeles is still only 6am in the morning. As a regular swimmer, she decides to go to the pool even though she feels very drowsy. Will her performance be affected?

In this situation, she may feel sluggish or evenly slightly moody but her actual performance for a moderate length and intensity training session will not be adversely affected. Her biggest challenge is to combat her mood which may lead to believe she has less energy. After exercise though, she is likely to feel more awake and ready to tackle the challenges of the day, probably also having built up a healthy appetite for a large West coast breakfast.

Why?

1. As she travelled in a Westerly direction, her chosen time to exercise is appropriate.
2. As she had some sleep, she will be able to achieve her normal levels of performance. Her mood might affect her level of enthusiasm though..

Case study

A married couple who are both crew are keen runners and are on joint rosters (work the same flights). They have just arrived home in London from a New York trip. They want to compete in the Windsor half marathon that afternoon but don't know how the flight and the sleep disruption will affect them. The female of the couple also wants to know if she will be more disadvantaged because of gender.

There is no reason that they cannot compete in the race that afternoon but neither are likely to achieve a personal best time. In endurance events sleep loss results in deterioration in performance. These effects are not gender specific. The degree that they affect them is more likely dependent on which of them is suffering from the most sleep deprivation rather than whether they are male or female.

Why?

1. Studies suggest that the effects of sleep deprivation apply equally to males and females.
2. Motor function such as those needed for running are less affected by sleep loss than tasks requiring fast reactions. Professional runners have however shown a tendency to be unwilling to maintain high levels of sustained performance when they are tired.
3. During the later part of a training session, performance can deteriorate after partial sleep deprivation.

Case study

A male crew member has completed his duty flying from London to Johannesburg. He has recently joined the gym and his fitness instructor has designed a program of weight orientated exercises for him. Each time he logs his achieved performance for each set of exercises in his training record book. He attends the gym straight away.

He may face two problems when trying to follow his training program. Sleep deprivation may make him feel that he isn't as strong as usual which may lead to motivational problems. He may become easily distracted and struggle to focus on the training tasks. Later, fatigue due to sleep deprivation may mean he can't match his usual weight targets.

Why?

1. As the departure and destination cities are in the same time zone, the timing of the exercise is not a factor.
2. Sleep deprivation from other duties may mean it is harder to maintain performance in repeated bouts and extended training sessions.
3. The perception that the training is harder than usual will mean that repeated sets suffer. In reality, maximum muscle

strength may not be affected by one night's sleep deprivation though it might not feel that way.

Tips for exercise

- Get some sleep before exercising.
- Choose an appropriate time to train; in the late afternoon if you are crossing time zones eastwards. Large transitions west mean morning exercise times are better.
- If you feel you are suffering from sleep deprivation, avoid strenuous exercise. A moderate or light routine may have beneficial effects.
- Recognise and remember that sleep deprivation does affect your performance and make allowances. Exercise is good for your health, but everything in moderation.

Conclusion

Sleep deprivation and disruption is a part of every day life for a crew member. The harsh reality is that very few shift workers compete in sport at high level. The varied and sometimes intrusive work schedules mean that crew members often struggle to balance competing responsibilities, including their sporting commitments. Top athletes benefit from a structured routine which can prove impossible for crew members to keep to. Managing how and when to exercise is a difficulty that will be faced by the active crew member. Keen sport enthusiasts who are thinking about joining the airline profession must be prepared to be flexible and creative with their training. It can be done and crew who are determined and dedicated will juggle these requirements. Clearly, the aircrew profession is a unique one with pressures that impact on all facets of life. The next chapter presents a brief overview of the historical developments within the aircrew profession. It then discusses the requirements for becoming either cabin crew or a pilot. Chapter 8 is primarily intended for those considering a career in the field. However, existing crew who are looking to work as recruitment representatives or to train pilots or cabin crew may also benefit from reading it.

CHAPTER EIGHT

Considering a career in the airline industry?

The roles of aircrew have changed in recent times from one of 'serving' passengers to one of 'safeguarding' them. This short chapter presents a brief history of the airline profession and the developments within it. For those interested in pursuing a career in the commercial airline industry as cabin crew or pilots, there is some detail about the recruitment process. The chapter is divided into the following sections:

- Historical developments within the aircrew profession
- The recruitment process for commercial airline crew
- The training period for crew
- Additional stages required to become a commercial airline pilot

History of the profession

In the early days of commercial aviation, the captain was in charge of the 'cockpit' while the co-pilot took responsibility for the cabin. This was in the days before the first 'stewardess' was employed and when she was, she was usually slim, tall, young, single, confident, and portrayed wealth and glamour to those who were wealthy enough to afford to travel. The stewardess was responsible for serving food, tea and coffee to passengers. Her communication with the pilots was limited to offering them a meal. Young attractive females tended to be the main types employed, but many were asked to leave as soon as they got married or became pregnant. At the time, the industry considered wedding bands or dependents as unglamorous and not befitting the jet set lifestyle of the growing industry. Pilots of the time were masculine and were tempted to arrogance by the many privileges associated with their professional status. The stereotypical idea of a pilot in the 1970's was that of a confident, charming, middle class man with a young wife. As a 'bread winner' for his family, he was well cared for with minimal domestic duties leaving him to enjoy life in a relaxed and comfortable environment.

The modern reality is quite different. Pilots and crew now work in a mass market, with airlines in competition with each other for business. Increasing stress levels are associated with the job. The focus of duties onboard has changed from serving to safeguarding the passengers by providing direction and expertise in case of emergencies—evacuations, onboard fire, hijacking, medical incidents, or to deal with unruly passengers. Some passengers, and the wider population, find it difficult to change their perception of aircrew from this gentle and service-minded image to a more skilled, authoritative group who might issue important instructions during safety procedures.

The changes seen by the industry have also affected crew who become the substitute fire brigade, police, and health care professionals for their passengers at 35.000 feet above the earth. Modern technology allows for immediate communication between the flight deck and ground based medical departments and security teams, but there is undeniably additional stress for people trying to juggle a multitude of roles onboard. The majority of flights are trouble free, and crew rarely need to call on their emergency training. It is easy for passengers to forget that crew are a highly trained group of people.

The recruitment process

Recruitment into the commercial airline industry involves a lengthy selection process. Flight crew are recruited in a different way to cabin crew. For pilots, their recruitment team is usually comprised of experienced pilots and psychologists with particular interests or specialisations (aviation, clinical, counselling or occupational psychologists to name a few). Each of the three major stages of pilot selection serves a distinct purpose. The first stage involves selection for entry to a pilot training program. This is usually funded by an airline organisation. Candidates who rely on self-funding will find it difficult to gain a place as competition is tough. It is the best interests of the sponsoring organisation to ensure that the participant is a good candidate as the training can be very expensive. The emphasis during selection is on factors associated with effective learning, adaptation to the airline industry, and keen cognitive and psychomotor skills required to operate an aircraft. Following training, the next stage is selection for employment by an airline or another commercial operator. There is no guarantee that once a pilot has received a flying license, they will be immediately employed. Individual airlines set their own standards for new recruits and trying to meet these requirements can be difficult. Pilots need to be in good physical shape too. In commercial aviation, they must have periodical medical checks to ensure they meet the requirements of the Joint Aviation Authority on Flight Crew Licensing. The medical team which carries out these assessments usually includes a doctor, a nurse and allied professionals as necessary. The purpose is to assess both the physical and mental wellbeing of new recruits and more established pilots. Most pilots are required to have this check once or twice a year, though the exact requirement depends on the airline. Regular training activities assess their technical, functional and management skills.

For cabin crew, airlines have their own specific models of recruitment. Formal requirements, set mainly for safety reasons, include being of a particular height, weight, with good vision, good hearing, and satisfying other health requirements. All recruits should be able to swim as this may be part of aircraft safety procedures in the unfortunate event of the aircraft making an emergency landing on water (*ditching*). Desirable skills include being able to speak more than one language or having some medical knowledge or experience of providing health care. Once an applicant has been short-listed for an interview, they are typically assessed on two levels with a primary focus on communication skills, decision making and sensitivity to passenger needs. Being able to effectively solve problems and to work as a team are also very important skills. Candidates are assessed while doing group based tasks which may simulate a safety or emergency related situation. During the second stage experienced cabin crew, human resource representatives, psychologists or a combination of these interview the candidates. The aim of the interview is to assess a candidate's level of motivation, independence, assertiveness, stress tolerance, ability to cooperate, and self-knowledge. In such a public facing role, physical presentation and personality are also important characteristics. Candidates who are successful at interview undergo training that teaches them about the statutory requirements of their role and provides them with safety and emergency training, aviation medicine, hijack/security procedures, restraining and breakaway techniques, and fire training. The training conforms to European statutory JAROPS standards (Joint Aviation Requirements Operations). Most courses also cover customer service training tailored to the way the airline strives to deal with passengers and the image they want to project. When training is complete, new recruits an existing team of professionals and are usually allocated to shorter routes (domestic or European destinations) first. Some smaller airlines may offer a combination of both short and long destinations whereas others adopt a senior based allocation system whereby new recruits are initially required to operate on shorter routes before he or she can request to become part of the long-haul team.

Although the identification of who is best suited in a selection process may depend upon the specific model advocated by the individual airline, a reliable selection process should try to assess the competence of applicants under simulated or actual pressures of team work. Organisations should dynamically evaluate the influence of personality traits on individual's capacities and skills for sustaining effective team work during periods of pressure and high work load. Undoubtedly, crew have a unique role to play at 35,000 feet. Successful hires will be those who can cope with the challenges of their work from early on in their employment.

Conclusion

Those who are considering a career as cabin crew or pilots may benefit from reading all chapters in this book which present the reality and pressures of this type of work and put some of the more glamorous associations in their real context. It will help to prepare you for the challenging aspects of a particularly unique career choice.

FURTHER READING

Ballard, T.J., Romito, P., Lauria, L., Vigilano, V., Caldora, M., Mazzanti, C. & Verdecchia, A. (2006). Self perceived health and mental health among women flight attendants. *Occupational and Environmental Medicine, 63*: pp. 33–38.

Bambaeichi, E., Reilly, T., Cable, N.T. & Giacomoni, M. (2005). The influence of time of day and partial sleep loss on muscle strength in eumenorrheic females. *Ergonomics, 48*: pp. 1499–1511.

Beck, A.T., Rush, A.J., Shaw, B.F. & Emery, G. (1979). *Cognitive Therapy of Depression.* New York: Guildford Press.

Bor, R., Field, G. & Scragg, P. (2002). The mental health of pilots: an overview of recent research. *Counselling Psychology Quarterly, 15*(3): pp. 239–256.

Bor, R. & Levitt, O. (2003). Air travel and the implications for Relationships. In: R. Bor. (Ed.). *Passanger Behaviour,* pp. 66–81. Aldershot: Ashgate.

Bor, R. & Hubbard, T. (2006). Introduction. In: R. Bor & T. Hubbard. (Eds.). *Aviation mental health; psychological implications for air transportation,* pp. 3–8. Aldershot: Ashgate.

Boyd, C. & Bain, P. (1997). *Once I get you up there, where the air is rarified: Health, Safety and The Working Conditions of airline Cabin Crew.* Oxford: Blackwell Publisher Ltd.

Caldwell, J. (1997). Fatigue in the aviation environment: an overview of the cause and effect as well as recommended countermeasures. *Aviation, Space, and Environmental Medicine, 68*: pp. 932–938.

Coleman, D. & Iso-Ahola, S.E. (1993). Leisure and Health; the role of social support and self-determination. *Journal of Leisure and Research, 25*: pp. 111–128.

Cooper, C. & Sloan, S. (1985b). The sources of stress in the wives of commercial airline pilots. *Aviation, Space, and Environmental Medicine, 56*: pp. 317–321.

Dallos, R. & Draper, R. (2000). *An introduction to Family Therapy: Systemic Theory and Practice.* Buckingham: Open University Press.

Eipstein, N. & Baucom, D. (2002). *Enhanced Cognitive Behavioural Therapy for Couples.* Washington DC: American Psychology Association.

Eriksen, C. (2006). How cabin crew deal with work stress. In: R. Bor & T. Hubbard. (Eds.). *Aviation mental health; psychological implications for air transportation,* pp. 209–227. Aldershot: Ashgate.

Eriksen, C. (2007). A qualitative investigation of cabin crews' experience of long haul travel; implications for coping style, psychological health, and personal, professional, and social relationships. *The British Library and London metropolitan University (awaiting publication).*

Ference, A. (2006). Psychological aspects of selection of flight attendant. In: R. Bor & T. Hubbard. (Eds.). *Aviation mental health; psychological implications for air transportation,* pp. 195–209. Aldershot: Ashgate.

Fleishman, J.A. (1984). Personality characteristics and coping patterns. *Journal of Health and Social Behaviour, 37*: pp. 229–244.

Gyllensten, K., Palmer, S. & Farrants, J. (2005). Perceptions of stress and stress interventions; overcoming resistance towards counselling. *Counselling Psychology Quarterly, 18*(1): pp. 19–29.

Gyllensten, K. & Palmer, S. (2005). Working with a client suffering from workplace stress in a primary care setting: A cognitive behavioural case study. *Counselling psychology Review, 20*(4): pp. 4–14.

Health and Safety Executive (2005). Stress related and Psychological disorder. Retrieved 18th of July 2007 from: www.hse.gov.uk.

Karlins, M., Koss, F. & McCully, L. (1989). The spousal factor in pilot stress. *Aviation, Space, and Environmental Medicine, 60*: pp. 1112–1115.

Lauria, L., Ballard, T.J., Corradi, L., Mazzanti, C., Scaravelli, G., Sgorbissa, F. & Verdecchia, A. (2004). Integrating Qualitative Methods into occupational health research: a study of women flight attendants. *Occupational and Environmental Medicine, 61*: pp. 163–166.

Levy, D.E., Faulkner, G.L., Dixon, R. (1984). Work and Family Interaction: The dual career family of the flight attendant. *Journal of Social Relations, 11*(2): pp. 67–88; USA Humboldt State University.

Meney, I., Waterhouse, J., Atkinson, G. & Davenne, D. (1998). The effect of one night's sleep deprivation in temperature, mood and physical performance in subjects with different amount of habitual activity. *Chronobiol Int, 15*: pp. 349–363.

Moos, R.H. & Schaefer, J.H. (1993). Coping recourses and Process; current concepts and measures. In: L. Goldberger & S. Breznitz (Eds.). *Handbook of Stress; theoretical and clinical aspects*, pp. 234–257. New York: Free Press.

Newy, C.A. & Hood, B.M. (2004). Determinants of shift-work adjustment for nursing staff: The critical experience of partners. *Journal of Professional Nursing, 20*(3): pp. 197–195.

Palmer, S. (2003). Stress management and prevention in the workplace. In: R. Woolfe, W. Dryden & S. Strawbridge (Eds.). *Handbook for Counselling Psychology*, pp. 572–591. London: Sage.

Partridge, C. & Goodman, T. (2006). Psychological problems among cabin crew. In: R. Bor & T. Hubbard. (Eds.). *Aviation mental health; psychological implications for air transportation*, pp. 227–239. Aldershot: Ashgate.

Pilcher, J. & Huffcutt, A.I. (1996). Effects of Sleep Deprivation on performance a meta-analysis. *Journal of Sleep*, pp. 318–326.

Reilly, T. & Pierce, M. (1994). The effects of partial sleep deprivation on weight-lifting performance. *Ergonomics*, 37: pp. 107–115.

Reilly, T. & Edwards, B. (2007). Altered sleep-wake cycles and physical performance in athletes. *Physiology and Behaviour*, 90(2–3): pp. 174–284.

Richards, P., Cleland, J. & Zuckerman, J. (2006). Psychological factors relating to physical health issues: how physical factors in aviation and travel affect psychological functioning. In: R. Bor & T. Hubbard. (Eds.). *Aviation mental health; psychological implications for air transportation*, pp. 27–39. Aldershot: Ashgate.

Seligman, M.E.P. & Csikszentmihalyi, M. (2000). Positive psychology; an introduction. *American Psychologist*, 55: pp. 5–14.

Sloan, S. & Cooper, C. (1986). Stress coping strategies in commercial airline pilots. *Journal of Occupational Medicine*, 23: pp. 49–52.

Snyder, C.P. & Lopez, S.J. (2002). *Handbook of positive psychology.* London: Oxford University Press.

Van Hooff, M.L.M., Gerts, S.A.E., Kompier, M.A.J. & Taris, T.W. (2007). Work-home inferences; how does it manifest itself from day to day? *Work and Stress*, 20(2): pp. 145–162.

Waterhouse, J., Edwards B., Atkinson, G., Reilly, T., Spencer, M. & Elsey, A. (2006). Occupational factors in pilot mental health: sleep loss, jetlag, and shift work. In: R. Bor & T. Hubbard. (Eds.). *Aviation mental health; psychological implications for air transportation*, pp. 209–227. Aldershot: Ashgate.

Waterhouse, J., Reilly, T. & Edwards, B. (2003). Long-Haul Flights, Travel Fatigue & Jet-Lag. In: R. Bor. (Ed.). *Passenger Behaviour*, pp. 246–260. Aldershot: Ashgate.

Wells, A. (2000). *Emotional Disorders and Meta cognition: Innovative Cognitive Therapy*. Chichester: John Wiley and Sons.